SCENES THAT HAPPEN

Dramatized snapshots about the real life of high schoolers

MARY KRELL-OISHI

MERIWETHER PUBLISHING LTD.
Colorado Springs, Colorado

Meriwether Publishing Ltd., Publisher
PO Box 7710
Colorado Springs, CO 80933-7710

Editor: Theodore O. Zapel
Cover design: Tom Myers

Printed in the United States of America
First Edition

Library of Congress Cataloging-in-Publication Data

Krell-Oishi, Mary, 1953-
Scenes that happen : dramatized snapshots about the real life of highschoolers / by Mary Krell-Oishi -- 1st ed.
p. cm.
Summary: Scenes for acting students to perform, based on high school experiences such as breaking up, peer pressure, dances, dating, cheating, telephones, and teenage pregnancy.
ISBN 10: 0-916260-79-8 ISBN 13: 9780916260798
1. High school students--Drama. 2. Young adult drama, American.
[1. High schools--Drama. 2. Schools--Drama. 3. Plays.] I. Title.
PS3561.R425S44 1991
812'.54--dc20 91-26778
CIP
AC

6 7 8 05 06 07

DEDICATION

For Harris, my Bunny
For Ricky, my Lamb
For my Mom and Dad, my heroes
And the kids at Sunny Hills, my friends

TABLE OF CONTENTS

PREFACE

When I was in my senior year of high school, my best friend, Marlene, begged me to ditch school with her. She pitched every argument, countered every one of my feeble excuses. In fact, most of my high school career was spent with Marlene and our co-best friend, Joe, getting in and out of trouble. But it was the normal kind of trouble. Homework, dating, parents.

In my fifteen years of teaching, I have seen myself over and over in my students. Being a teen is a unique experience, and every occurrence, no matter how trivial to an adult, is a major event in a young life. It is for those teens that I write. The everyday kid. The one who says each morning, "Please, God, don't let me look like a jerk today at school."

I hope that young actors today can see a little of themselves in these scenes. I write scenes for my drama students, "my kids" because there is a need for them to take something close to their own lives and make it truly become a full character. Eventually some of them may take on Willy Loman or Blanche Dubois, but until then, try the characters in this book . . . and most of all have fun!

Mary Krell-Oishi

P.S. Mom, Marlene and I had a great time at the beach.

INTRODUCTION

Mary Krell-Oishi is a careful observer of the young people who surround her in her life as a high school teacher. She has taken advantage of her observations to write a wide variety of scenes that reflect the lives, attitudes and concerns of her students.

These scenes provide opportunities for young people to play roles that intersect with their own experience. Some of the scenes deal with serious issues, such as teenage pregnancy, peer pressure and young love, while others offer light-hearted looks at the everyday concerns of young people. Across the board, they celebrate the kind of friendship that makes adolescence bearable and memorable.

The scenes can be presented individually or put together into an evening of entertainment. They can be used as audition pieces or classroom exercises or to prompt discussion about specific issues. Or they can simply be performed for the sheer pleasure that comes from exploring theatrical possibilities. However they may be used, these scenes will provide pleasure, provoke thought and stimulate the imaginations of both performers and audiences.

John Glore, Literary Manager of Tony Award-Winning South Coast Repertory, Costa Mesa, California, and author of the children's plays, *Wind of a Thousand Tales* and *Folktales Too.*

· GIRLS ·

BEACHING IT

MARLENE: Ready at all times to have fun.

MARY: Ready to have fun, just not at all times.

SETTING: Scene opens at school; a warm day, in quad area. Both girls are seniors; it is late September.

MARLENE: *(At a run, she grabs MARY by the arm.)* **We're outa here girl. Let's go.**

MARY: What?

MARLENE: Beach bound, we are beaching it today.

MARY: Now?

MARLENE: I love the present, why wait for the future?

MARY: Because in the present, we both have classes to go to.

MARLENE: Those classes will still be here tomorrow, the next day, the day after that, right up until that glorious day in June when we are declared free.

MARY: You might get declared free sooner than June if you start cutting classes this early in the year.

MARLENE: Girl, get a life. It's probably the last warm day of this year . . . If we don't take advantage of it now, if we don't grab it, live it, it will be gone.

MARY: Please.

MARLENE: I'm serious. We need to get out of here. I need to get out of here.

MARY: We've got class.

MARLENE: *(Tempting her)* **Joe's going.**

MARY: Where?

MARLENE: Well, I can guarantee you, not to class.

MARY: To the beach? With us?

MARLENE: Yes to both questions.

MARY: Omigod. Joe Morrow at the beach . . . in nothing but those white shorts.

MARLENE: Nothing but those white shorts and that

dark tanned skin, taut over rippling muscles.

MARY: *(Losing herself in the vision)* **The ocean water trickling over him . . . the blue of the sky reflected in the blue of his eyes.**

MARLENE: The sunlight caught in his hair. His powerful body straining against the waves, coming closer to shore, to us, waiting there for him.

MARY: And me . . . in a bathing suit my mother picked out for me. No way. I am class bound.

MARLENE: Darn! I almost had you. C'mon, go with us.

MARY: Go without me. What's the big deal?

MARLENE: You have the car.

MARY: Very nice. What a good friend you are.

MARLENE: It's more than that, and you know it.

MARY: Marlene, the bell is going to ring, and WE are going to be late.

MARLENE: That is impossible.

MARY: How is it impossible?

MARLENE: You can't be late for something you have no intention of going to.

MARY: Fine, you go to the beach. I'm going to class.

MARLENE: You know, I have put up with this goody two shoes attitude from you for the last three years. Snap out of it.

MARY: I'm not going.

MARLENE: What is the deal here?

MARY: I'll get caught.

MARLENE: So, what are they gonna do? Spank you?

MARY: You lose a unit for every three cuts.

MARLENE: This is your first cut . . . in ALL THREE YEARS SO FAR!

MARY: I'll get in trouble.

MARLENE: No you won't.

MARY: Yes, I will. I always get caught doing this kind of thing.

MARLENE: What kind of thing?

MARY: Like the time you talked me into playing Destructo at the store.

MARLENE: What? What are you talking about . . .?

MARY: When you talked me into dive bombing our fingers into the candy bars at Vons. I got caught and you didn't and I got in trouble.

MARLENE: For heaven's sake, that was when we were eight years old.

MARY: There have been other times I can bring up.

MARLENE: Like when?

MARY: Like the time you talked me into going over to John Lee's house . . .

MARLENE: Never mind. Geez, you never forget anything, do you?

MARY: I try to keep in mind past history so I won't repeat it.

MARLENE: Listen to me. Even if we do get caught, you won't get in trouble. They will blame me for talking you into such a horrible crime, they will say how disappointed they are in you and, at worst, you'll get a detention. Not a bad price to pay to see Joe Morrow at the beach one last time before he starts to wear long pants and sweaters.

MARY: Detention, huh?

MARLENE: One lousy little detention.

MARY: What's it like?

MARLENE: Loser city. Take a book, keep to yourself, don't make eye contact with anyone. You'll be fine.

MARY: Joe is going for sure?

MARLENE: Uh huh.

MARY: I've only got Art and English Comp coming up.

MARLENE: Sheesh . . . You're cutting two lousy little classes. I've been gone the whole day.

MARY: Marlene . . . what is wrong with you?

MARLENE: We'll discuss my lack of discipline at the beach.

MARY: I am getting an A in both classes.

MARLENE: You're getting A's in all of your classes. It's your senior year. Live a little.

MARY: *(Looking at her)* **You won't ask me to do this again, will you?**

MARLENE: I promise.

MARY: OK.

MARLENE: YES!

MARY: But not again. I'm not cutting class again to go to the beach.

MARLENE: Never. *(Taking MARY's arm, leading her out.)* **Ski season, however, is fast approaching.** *(Looking around)* **RUN!!**

BORROWING

JAN: Age 17, attractive, older sister.

SUZI: Age 15, also attractive.

SETTING: Jan's bedroom.

SUZI: *(Heading for the closet)* **Hey, Jan.**

JAN: *(Without looking up.)* **Hi.** *(Notices SUZI rummaging through closet.)* **What are you doing?**

SUZI: Getting the grey jacket with the silver buttons. You know, the one I always wear with my black jeans.

JAN: You mean the one that you always take without asking to wear with your black jeans?

SUZI: *(In closet)* **Yeah, that's the one . . .**

JAN: You know, just once I wish you would ask before you take.

SUZI: Jan, the times I've worn it, you haven't been home to ask.

JAN: I'm home now.

SUZI: OK, fine. Can I please borrow your jacket?

JAN: No.

SUZI: Very funny. Is it in here or in the hall closet?

JAN: It's in there, but don't bother, because you can't wear it.

SUZI: You're kidding.

JAN: No, I'm not. I'm getting tired of always finding my clothes in your closet. Some of them I haven't even worn yet.

SUZI: Oh, come on. You borrow my clothes just as much as I do yours.

JAN: Oh, yes. All the oversized jackets I can use.

SUZI: You can use anything of mine you want to use. No one is stopping you.

JAN: Only the fact that I'm a size eight and you're a

size six. It really bugs me that my clothes fit you and yours just manage to be too small for me.

SUZI: Oh, I see. I'm at fault here because I'm smaller than you. God, you act like you're fat or something.

JAN: No, I know I'm not. It just bugs me that you have twice of my size wardrobe because you have your clothes and mine as well.

SUZI: So I can belt and tie your clothes. I'm sorry. Forgive me for being a size smaller than you.

JAN: Just go to your own closet and get your own clothes.

SUZI: You're really not going to let me borrow that jacket?

JAN: You know, maybe if you'd learn to ask instead of just take all the time, I would.

SUZI: OK, please? It won't happen again. I will ask from now on.

JAN: No.

SUZI: I can't believe this. You are being such a bitch.

JAN: Just stay out of my closet.

SUZI: Fine.

JAN: And stay out of my room.

SUZI: No problem. And listen . . .

JAN: What?

SUZI: Just stay out of my life.

JAN: Well, I'm devastated.

SUZI: I can't believe you're acting like this over a stupid jacket.

JAN: Believe it.

SUZI: There's got to be more to it than this . . .

JAN: Honestly? No. There isn't. Hard to believe, precious sister, that I am genuinely tired of you and your demands?

SUZI: What demands?

JAN: It's never "Jan, may I borrow?" or "Jan, would you

mind if I used . . ." It's always just take, take, take.

SUZI: God, back off. You are really overreacting.

JAN: Overreacting to you. Finally reacting to me. Just leave my stuff alone.

SUZI: You're really serious, aren't you?

JAN: You finally figured that out? I work and earn money for most everything I own in that closet. I don't want you just rummaging through it. I'm serious, yes.

SUZI: I'm really sorry, Jan. I didn't realize that you truly felt this way.

JAN: Well, I do.

SUZI: You should have told me this sooner. We're sisters, and I love you. I wouldn't hurt you.

JAN: I know. It's just that I kept it bottled up and I just exploded at once. I'm sorry, too.

SUZI: I'll ask from now on, OK?

JAN: Thanks. *(Hugs SUZI.)*

SUZI: Is it OK if I borrow that grey jacket?

JAN: No.

SUZI: What? What was all this true confessions stuff we just had? I thought everything was fine between us.

JAN: It is, but that doesn't mean you can borrow my jacket.

SUZI: You are such a bitch.

JAN: Get out of my room.

SUZI: Fine. I hate you!

JAN: Who cares!

SUZI: I don't want your lousy jacket anyway.

JAN: Good, 'cause you're not getting it. And stay out of all of my things.

THE DANCE

MARY: At sixteen, is anticipating her first formal dance, and is quite excited about it at first.

RENE: At seventeen, is Mary's best friend and is trying to set her straight on the ways of men.

RENE: So, Mary. Tell me all. I heard what happened today in class.

MARY: Oh, Rene, it was so neat. I was just sitting there and in comes Carrie, carrying this big balloon with carnations and a card. I couldn't believe it.

RENE: So, what did the card say?

MARY: Wait, I've got it right here. I swear, John is just a really neat person.

RENE: He's sweet. What did you do when you got it?

MARY: I was dying for class to end, so I could find him and tell him yes.

RENE: So, you're going with him?

MARY: Oh, definitely. We will have such a great time.

RENE: Totally.

MARY: Here's the card. OK, read it.

RENE: Let me see. *(Reading to herself)* **Hmm hmm hmm. Oh, that is sweet. He is funny. Like Homecoming is no big deal for you. I love it.** *(Reading on)* **Uh oh.**

MARY: What, uh oh?

RENE: Did you see this last part?

MARY: What?

RENE: Love, John.

MARY: So?

RENE: He does know that you guys will be going as just friends, doesn't he?

MARY: Of course . . . at least I think so.

RENE: Are you sure?

MARY: Oh, come on, he's got to know that. I mean, we've known each other for so long and have partied and stuff, but he knows that it's just as friends.

RENE: "Love, John."

MARY: Rene, you're making more of this than it is.

RENE: You think so?

MARY: Of course.

RENE: Don't you guys talk on the phone a lot?

MARY: Yes. Almost every night.

RENE: Every night?

MARY: He's just a friend. We have a lot in common. He knows that I could never be interested in him that way.

RENE: Don't you think you should make that clear to him?

MARY: What am I going to say? Hey John, don't forget, we're "just friends" OK?

RENE: Yes.

MARY: Oh, please. That would be stupid. Besides, it's implying things that may not even be there.

RENE: Fine, Mary, you do what you want . . . but if it were me, I'd get it straight before you tell him you'll go.

MARY: Uh oh.

RENE: You already told him?

MARY: Right after class was over, I ran to his class and caught him and told him yes. I was so excited that he would take such time to ask me so sweetly.

RENE: You ran?

MARY: Well, I was excited.

RENE: You're an idiot. Look at that . . . "love, John."

MARY: Oh dear . . .

RENE: Well, that's one way of putting it.

MARY: What do you think I should do?

RENE: I think you better tell him as soon as possible.

MARY: Yeah. What should I say?

RENE: Just be honest. Tell him you like him as a friend and that's it.

MARY: That sounds so cold.

RENE: Not as cold as getting his hopes up.

MARY: But what if he didn't mean it like you think?

RENE: Here's what you do. Are you going to talk to him tonight?

MARY: I usually talk to him about 9:30.

RENE: Every night?

MARY: Yes.

RENE: Oh, brother. OK, here's what you say. You say how nice it is that we are going as friends and that you feel so good that it is him you're going with, 'cause you know you'll have a good time with such a good friend. You got that so far?

MARY: I'm not an idiot, Rene.

RENE: Right. Anyway, then you have to give him an out. If you sense that he is feeling funny about it, tell him you will understand if he doesn't want to take just a friend. That way if he feels like he is getting dumped on, then you, as a friend, will be giving him the option to ask someone else.

MARY: OK, so what if he says it is fine?

RENE: Then go. As long as it is clear, up front, that he knows that it is just as friends.

MARY: That sounds good. I just don't want to come off like a bitch, you know?

RENE: If he is as good a friend as you say he is, then you will come out looking like a great person. If he is a jerk, then you are in for trouble.

MARY: What do you mean?

RENE: Well, if his male ego is pierced, then you are out of luck with him.

MARY: He won't be like that . . . I think.

RENE: Call me tonight right after you talk to him and we'll talk, OK?

MARY: OK. God, all of a sudden I'm not excited anymore. I feel like this is going to be more work than fun.

RENE: Hey, the ball is in his court after this. It will be fine if he acts like a mature adult.

MARY: We're talking a 17-year-old male.

RENE: You might be in trouble.

MARY: Oh, not with John. He's too nice. He'll be fine about this. Trust me.

RENE: I hope so. Because if he likes you more than you like him and you shut him down, he is going to be a jerk about it.

MARY: Not John.

RENE: He's a man, isn't he?

MARY: Uh oh.

RENE: Uh oh is right. *(They share a look.)* **You better call me the minute you get off the phone with him, do you understand?**

MARY: Don't worry, I will.

RENE: I'll see ya later, OK?

MARY: Yeah. Oh, and Rene?

RENE: Yes?

MARY: Thanks.

RENE: No problem. Call me.

MARY: I will. *(By herself)* **Damn.**

GIRL TALK

TRICIA: Bubbly, a bit pushy.

LEAH: Quieter, unsure of herself.

SETTING: A nice public bathroom. The girls are discussing their dates.

TRICIA: *(Speaking as she enters)* **So, what do you think of Bob? Are you in love or what?**

LEAH: Tricia, I just met him. For goodness sake, give me some time here.

TRICIA: I know, but isn't he the cutest thing you ever saw in your life?

LEAH: He's OK.

TRICIA: OK? Leah, are you nuts? He's wonderful. He's funny, he's good looking, he's well built, he's smart. What's not to like?

LEAH: Tricia, I don't know. He's just not . . .

TRICIA: He's not James.

LEAH: I didn't say that.

TRICIA: You don't have to. I can see it on your face.

LEAH: I'm sorry, but I can't help it.

TRICIA: You're an idiot.

LEAH: Yeah, well.

TRICIA: You know, I don't know why I keep on trying to help you. It's a complete waste of time. Hand me that lipstick.

LEAH: Here. I never asked you to do it, you know.

TRICIA: I know. But as your best friend, it is my duty to try and help you get over that joke of a relationship you were in and move you on to someone better.

LEAH: Than James?

TRICIA: Leah, my cat is better than James, and he's been neutered. Which, come to think of it, wouldn't hurt James a bit.

LEAH: Triciaaa. No, really. I don't understand why you don't like James. He never did anything to you.

TRICIA: Well, like the song says, "Girlfriend, what has he done for you lately?"

LEAH: It's not his fault that he's not here. He got a scholarship to Berkeley. What's he supposed to do? Say, "Oh, no, sorry, Dad. I have to turn down your offer to pay for all of my college up north. You see, my girlfriend is still in high school down in Fullerton, so I'll just wait until she graduates and go to Fullerton JC until then."

TRICIA: That's not what I mean, and you know it. I don't expect you to drop him 'cause he's not here. I . . . and all of your true friends, by the way . . . expect you not to become a nun.

LEAH: I have to be faithful.

TRICIA: *(Picking up LEAH's hand)* Let me see. No, no, I don't see a ring on that finger.

LEAH: Well, *(Taking her hand back)* that's just a matter of time.

TRICIA: Listen, idiot, that may very well be, but until then, have a good time.

LEAH: But . . .

TRICIA: No buts. You can't honestly stand there and tell me you think that James is sitting home every evening waiting for the moment you call, do you?

LEAH: I . . .

TRICIA: In fact, I bet if you called him right now, he wouldn't even be home.

LEAH: So, what if he's not. He's probably at the library studying or something.

TRICIA: Try the "or something."

LEAH: Besides, what am I going to say? "Hi, James, I'm here at the Velvet Turtle, yes, our place, on a date. I just wanted to check on you"? Very cool.

TRICIA: You don't have to tell him you're on a date, or even where you are. Just call and see.

LEAH: No.

TRICIA: Afraid?

LEAH: No.

TRICIA: Then do it.

LEAH: No.

TRICIA: That's what I thought.

LEAH: Think what you like. Besides, like you said, there is no ring on his finger, either.

TRICIA: Then why won't you give Bob a chance?

LEAH: I don't know. He's not my type.

TRICIA: Oh, yes, I can understand that. I can see how an intelligent, good looking, well-built senior considering a full ACADEMIC scholarship to Stanford wouldn't compare to James and his ITT technical institute aspirations.

LEAH: That's not fair. You know that James wants to be a computer repair person. They make very good money.

TRICIA: So do doctors. Which is what Bob is going to be. After, of course, he finishes his professional football career, which he has been scouted for.

LEAH: I know, I know. Bob is perfect, Bob is wonderful. James is just a cog in the big wheel of life. But I love him.

TRICIA: Call him. see if he's there.

LEAH: NO!

TRICIA: What are you afraid of?

LEAH: Fine, I'll call.

TRICIA: Good, here's the phone.

LEAH: *(Dialing)* **This is stupid. It's not going to prove anything at all.**

TRICIA: Just call.

LEAH: It's ringing . . . and ringing . . . and ringing . . .

TRICIA: And ringing.

LEAH: Where the hell is he?

TRICIA: Probably studying . . . hee hee hee.

LEAH: That little . . . Oh, hello?

TRICIA: He's there?

LEAH: *(Shushing TRICIA)* **Hi, James. Where were you? . . . Studying?** *(To TRICIA)* **See, I told you.** *(Back to JAMES)* **No, nothing, I just missed you. Where . . . . uh, oh, Tricia and I went out to dinner. Oh, I'll tell her hi for you . . . This weekend? Of course I'll be home. Where do you think? On a date? Ha ha.**

TRICIA: Oh, please, I'm getting ill.

LEAH: Will you shut up? Oh, no, James, not you. Yes, well, my mom will be very surprised to see this call on her credit card bill, so I better go. I love you, too. Yeah, see you Friday. James, we have to talk, OK? OK. Bye.

TRICIA: Well, the rest of this evening is going to be great fun, I can tell. You'll be mooning over James, Bob will be mooning over you, and Tom and I will eat everyone's dessert.

LEAH: No, it will be fine. Bob is kind of cute, isn't he?

TRICIA: What? Didn't you just tell James you loved him?

LEAH: Yeah, but for the first time, it didn't come naturally. I felt like I HAD to say it, you know? Something was missing when I just spoke to him.

TRICIA: What? Magic? Romance? Karma?

LEAH: No, silence.

TRICIA: Silence?

LEAH: Yeah, there were voices in the background. Female voices.

TRICIA: Uh oh. Maybe they live in the dorm.

LEAH: It's an all male dorm.

TRICIA: Uh oh. Are you OK?

LEAH: Yes. I feel sad that I'm not mad. I'm not

anything . . . except maybe hungry. Let's go back to the table.

TRICIA: You are so strange.

LEAH: Yeah, I know. So, Bob is going on a full scholarship to Stanford? Is he taking those incredibly broad shoulders with him?

TRICIA: Nasty girl. *(They exit, laughing.)*

GROWING UP

LIZ: Age 17

AMY: Age 14

SETTING: Kitchen, late morning. Amy is preparing breakfast for herself. Liz enters, glances at her sister Amy, ignores her and begins to prepare herself something to eat. Amy is blocking the bread, Liz reaches in front of her to get it, shoving her on the shoulder in the process.

AMY: I hope I'm not in your way here. *(LIZ ignores her.)* **Fine, whatever. You don't have to talk to me.**

LIZ: I have no intention of talking to you at all.

AMY: Fine. I don't want to talk to you either.

LIZ: Then don't.

AMY: I won't.

LIZ: Good. *(They eat in silence for a minute or two.)*

AMY: So, how long are you going to be mad at me? *(LIZ ignores her.)* **Liz, how long?**

LIZ: Mmmmonnnow *(This is "I don't know" mumbled.)*

AMY: Whatever. I don't care.

LIZ: Good.

AMY: I don't, you know. You can be mad at me for as long as you want, and I really won't care at all. I know I was right, and that is all that matters. So you be mad. You stay mad forever if that's what you want. I honestly don't care.

LIZ: Then why don't you shut up?

AMY: Fine, I will.

LIZ: Fine, do it.

AMY: I will. I don't have to talk to you either.

LIZ: Then don't.

AMY: I won't.

LIZ: *(Slamming her glass on the table, yelling)* **GOOD!** *(They sit in silence, AMY watching LIZ wipe up the drink she has spilled.)*

AMY: Do you want me to apologize?

LIZ: Amy, I just want you to shut up.

AMY: I'm sorry. Really.

LIZ: Uh huh.

AMY: I didn't know you liked him, honestly. He just came over and I was nice to him while you weren't here. He said that you two were going to study together. He didn't say it was a date.

LIZ: It wasn't a date.

AMY: Then why are you so mad?

LIZ: Because it was supposed to turn into a date.

AMY: Well, why didn't you tell me?

LIZ: Because I didn't realize at the time that I had a mantrap for a younger sister who would steal a man right from under my nose.

AMY: I didn't steal him. I just . . . borrowed him.

LIZ: Like my jacket? You never returned that either.

AMY: I can't help it if we hit it off. I can't help it that he likes me.

LIZ: Whatever.

AMY: If you say "whatever" to me one more time, I swear . . .

LIZ: What, you'll hit me? Well, you'll have to beat me to it.

AMY: I can't stand it when you are like this.

LIZ: Whatever.

AMY: You . . . *(She goes to hit LIZ. LIZ, as promised, beats her to it. They struggle around the kitchen, over chairs, table, various other things.)* **I hate you! You are a selfish, inconsiderate tramp!**

LIZ: *(Over her)* **You are lower than low. You are the worst kind of rotten excuse for a human being.** *(The fight ends with them on the floor. They are lying among the various things they have run over and around during the fight.)*

AMY: Well, this is mature. *(She laughs.)*

LIZ: We are growing up to be the finest of young women, I must say.

AMY: *(Releasing LIZ from her grasp.)* **I really am sorry about John. I didn't know that you liked him like that.**

LIZ: I don't. *(She smiles.)*

AMY: You don't? *(LIZ shakes her head "no.")* **Then why am I covered with cereal and milk?**

LIZ: Because you're you.

AMY: Excuse me?

LIZ: Listen. For the last few years, it's been me the guys come over to see. You were always just my little sister who was always hanging around. Now, it's different.

AMY: You mean now I'm competition?

LIZ: Let's not get carried away, OK? No, what I mean is that now, you're not that "little kid," you know, Liz's sister. Now, you're growing up.

AMY: I know.

LIZ: What's really hard is that you're growing up pretty. The scraped knees and buck teeth are gone.

AMY: Yeah, now they're all covered with Fruit Loops.

LIZ: I have a feeling that this new, grown-up pretty you is going to take some getting used to.

AMY: I'm ready for it.

LIZ: You may be . . . it's going to take me a while. *(They hug, and start to clean up.)* **In the meantime . . .**

AMY: Yeah . . .?

LIZ: Leave anyone over the age of 17 alone until you've cleared him with me.

AMY: You got it.

I'M FINE, REALLY

JULIE: Age 16, a sweet lively girl who is concerned for her friend's welfare.

TRACI: Age 16, in love with Alan and blind to his faults and mistreatment of her.

JULIE: Traci, where were you last night? I thought you and Alan were going to come over after the game.

TRACI: Poor Alan. He felt so bad after losing the game that he just wanted to go home and be alone.

JULIE: Well, it's not like he lost it all by himself. There are quite a few other guys on the football team.

TRACI: Not all of them dropped the ball in the last few seconds of the game on the two yard line when the team is behind by only three points.

JULIE: I see what you mean. So what did you do?

TRACI: We just went to his house. His parents are away for the weekend, so we just stayed over there.

JULIE: Oh. Well, too bad. You missed a great party.

TRACI: Julie, you know how Alan gets when he's depressed. The last thing he wants is to be around a bunch of people having a good time.

JULIE: Yeah, I guess so. Kind of a drag for you, though, isn't it?

TRACI: What does that mean?

JULIE: Nothing. Except he seems depressed a lot lately.

TRACI: He's not. He just has some things going on in his life right now that trouble him.

JULIE: So he becomes a hermit?

TRACI: He's not a hermit. He's just sensitive. He says that I am the only one who understands how he feels. He needs me, Julie.

JULIE: I guess so. Well, c'mon, we're going to be late for class if we don't hurry.

TRACI: **Yeah, I'm coming. Let me get my books, OK?**

JULIE: **Traci, you are always late for everything. Hurry up. I'll just drag you there and you won't be late.** *(She laughingly grabs her arm and drags her a few steps.)*

TRACI: **Ow! Hey!** *(She pulls away.)*

JULIE: **God, I barely touched you. What a crybaby.** *(TRACI is trying to cover up real pain.)* **Traci . . . what's wrong?**

TRACI: **Nothing, I just whacked my arm on the car door this weekend and it still hurts.**

JULIE: **Let me see.**

TRACI: **Julie, it's fine. C'mon, we're going to be late.**

JULIE: **Let me see your arm, Traci.**

TRACI: **I'm fine. Let's go.**

JULIE: *(Pulling up TRACI's sleeve, seeing a large bruise.)* **What the heck is this?**

TRACI: **I told you.**

JULIE: **This is not from hitting your arm on the car door. This looks like it was slammed in a car door.**

TRACI: **Are you calling me a liar?**

JULIE: **I'm asking you a question. How did this happen?**

TRACI: **I told you.**

JULIE: **Look at me, Traci. I've been your best friend since seventh grade, and I know when you are not telling the truth, so talk to me. What happened?**

TRACI: **If I tell you, you won't act stupid about it?**

JULIE: **Did your dad hit you?**

TRACI: **Oh, c'mon, Julie. You know my dad. No.**

JULIE: *(Extremely relieved)* **Oh, thank God. Well, what then?**

TRACI: **It's just so stupid. Alan and I were wrestling around and my arm hit the table next to the couch.**

JULIE: *(Quietly, disbelieving)* **What?**

TRACI: **You know how Alan likes to play with me. Well, he was so down after Friday's game that I wanted**

to get him in a good mood, so I started teasing with him.

JULIE: And . . . .

TRACI: Well, he started to laugh and play back and then I whacked my arm on the table and that was the end of play time.

JULIE: And that was all?

TRACI: Yes, that was all.

JULIE: Isn't that what happened when you chipped your front tooth?

TRACI: What?

JULIE: You said the exact same thing about your front tooth getting chipped. You said that you and Alan were wrestling on the floor and you accidentally got whacked in the mouth.

TRACI: You know he likes to play.

JULIE: Playing a little rough, aren't we?

TRACI: I really don't think it's any of your business.

JULIE: What about last month when you said that you ran into the door and got a black eye. *(TRACI looks away.)* **It's Alan, isn't it? He hits you.**

TRACI: He doesn't hit me.

JULIE: Talk to me, Traci.

TRACI: *(Very quietly)* **Alan gets upset, and he needs me. I have to be there for him.**

JULIE: You mean he needs a punching bag, so you're it?

TRACI: *(Gathers her things.)* **I knew you wouldn't understand.**

JULIE: *(Stopping her)* **Traci, I'm trying to. Tell me. Don't shut me out.**

TRACI: Like Friday after the game. I wanted to go to the party and he didn't want to. He knew that Brian and Pat and the rest of the guys would make fun of him for dropping the ball and losing the game. I kept bugging him about going. It was my own fault.

JULIE: What? Omigod. I can't believe you just said that.

TRACI: But he told me to shut up. I wouldn't let up.

JULIE: So he hits you? Just because you speak?

TRACI: He didn't hit me. He just held me.

JULIE: Traci, you are 5'2" and he is 6'1". I can see it. He picked you up and shook you like a cat.

TRACI: He didn't mean to. He never does.

JULIE: What do you mean, "He never does"? He does this a lot?

TRACI: Not every day. You make it sound worse than it is.

JULIE: Has he ever full out hit you?

TRACI: No, he would never do that. I'd have to get him very, very angry for him to do that. No, I know when not to push him.

JULIE: I cannot believe I am hearing this out of an intelligent human being. He has no right.

TRACI: He doesn't mean to.

JULIE: If he is grabbing you now, the next step is going to be hitting.

TRACI: He won't. He loves me.

JULIE: Oh, fine. I'd hate to see it if he hated you. That's just sick, Traci —

TRACI: *(Cutting her off)* And I love him.

JULIE: And that is sicker.

TRACI: Julie, don't say another word. Not another word.

JULIE: Word, heck, I've got paragraphs to say...I could speak volumes.

TRACI: If you value our friendship, you will forget this conversation ever took place.

JULIE: I do value our friendship. And I value you. Obviously more than you do.

TRACI: You don't understand. Alan needs me. He needs my love.

JULIE: He needs someone to punish for his own stupid life.

TRACI: Goodbye Julie. *(She begins to go.)*

JULIE: He needs help, Traci.

TRACI: *(Stopping, but without looking back)* **He needs me.** *(She is gone.)*

JULIE: *(Sadly, quietly)* **Traci . . .** *(She looks after her friend.)*

MIDNIGHT RUN

MARCI: At 16, she is excited and adventuresome as well as in lust with Jason. Willing to risk reputation to see him.

NICOLE: Also 16, but reluctantly joining Marci on her little quest to see Jason.

SETTING: The scene takes place on a boy's front yard. The bushes are indicated by using chairs.

MARCI: *(Enters crawling on all fours, skulking close to the ground. She makes it to about Down-stage Left of Center, her head pops up, then she quickly drops down again. She whispers.)* **This is great. I can see his bedroom light from here.** *(MARCI looks behind her and sees she is alone.)* **Nicole, will you get over here?**

NICOLE: *(NICOLE enters crawling in the same way MARCI was.)* **Marci, this is the stupidest, most ridiculous thing you have ever gotten me into. And you have gotten me into quite a few ridiculous and stupid things.**

MARCI: Stay down and be quiet.

NICOLE: Bugs. Everywhere there are bugs. And I'm covered with dirt. This is just great.

MARCI: *(Looking upward)* **I can't see anything, can you?**

NICOLE: Just the leaves in my eyes. What kind of bush is this, anyway?

MARCI: He's gotta be home. I see a light.

NICOLE: I bet this is some kind of ragweed. I know it. I'm going to blow up like a balloon tomorrow. A big, red, rash covered balloon.

MARCI: *(Completely ignoring NICOLE's complaints.)* **Look, look, there he is. It's Jason.**

NICOLE: How do you know that's him?

MARCI: Look at those shoulders. Who do you think those belong to, his mother? Hand me my binoculars.

NICOLE: And why do I always have to carry all the supplies on your stupid little excursions into the land of felony?

MARCI: Because you carry a big purse. Quick, before he goes.

NICOLE: We could get in so much trouble. I'm not kidding, you know. This is a felony. Peeping Toms. Voyeurism. It's almost perverted to be doing this, Marci.

MARCI: OK, OK, so we're teenage perverts.

NICOLE: If we get caught, I swear, I'll just die. My mother will die. My whole family will die.

MARCI: So you'll save money with a group rate funeral. Oh, he's near the window. Yes, come closer, baby. *(They both have their binoculars out and look up.)*

NICOLE: My goodness, his shoulders are almost obscenely broad, aren't they? *(The two girls watch for a moment in silent admiration.)*

NICOLE: OK, we've seen him. Now let's go before anyone sees us.

MARCI: Not yet.

NICOLE: What do you mean, "Not yet"? How long are we going to stay here?

MARCI: Until I see him naked.

NICOLE: *(Rising)* **NAKED?**

MARCI: *(Pulling her down)* **Are you crazy? Do you want people to notice us?**

NICOLE: *(Instantly dropping)* **You think we won't be noticed now crouching here in Jason's bush? . . . Wait a minute, that's not what I meant.** *(They both break into dirty laughter.)*

MARCI: And you say I'm evil.

NICOLE: You KNOW what I meant.

MARCI: And so does Sigmund Freud.

NICOLE: You can read filth into the most innocent statements.

MARCI: Who's the one who has been muttering things all night like pervert and voyeurism and peeping Tom? I'm just here to look.

NICOLE: Fine, fine, whatever. You came to look, you saw him, now let's go.

MARCI: *(Getting up, looking around the yard.)* **I want a souvenir.**

NICOLE: First you want to see him naked, and now you want a souvenir? And I'm the pervert?

MARCI: Listen, Nicole, he's gotta shower sometime. And look up there, to the right of his bedroom window. That's his bathroom. I just know it is. If we wait long enough, he's sure to go in there.

NICOLE: Marci, the window is frosted. There are curtains over it. You won't be able to see anything.

MARCI: But maybe I will be able to see an outline. *(She wiggles her eyebrows suggestively.)*

NICOLE: You are a pig. *(She suddenly becomes alert.)* **What was that?**

MARCI: *(Diving back behind the "chairs")* **I don't know.** *(They both drop and wait, then MARCI slowly looks up.)* **Omigod!**

NICOLE: What? Who was it?

MARCI: It was your mom's car.

NICOLE: No way. Did she see us?

MARCI: I don't think so. Wait, is she slowing? *(They pause for a moment.)* **No, no. She's gone.**

NICOLE: That's all, brother. I'm gone. Lets go. *(She begins to pack up the binoculars and crawl off.)*

MARCI: But I haven't seen him naked.

NICOLE: Have you completely lost your mind? You drag me here to hide in God knows what kind of poison bushes, I'm covered with dirt, bugs are crawling down my bra, I'm carrying around my father's 200 dollar binoculars. We've peeped at an

innocent guy through his bedroom window as my mother drives by and almost sees us doing all of this, and now you want to see him NAKED?

MARCI: We've come this far, why stop short of a goal? Shoot for the stars, Nicole.

NICOLE: I'm going to just plain shoot if we don't leave right now.

MARCI: All right. But I want a souvenir.

NICOLE: ***Now*, Marci.**

MARCI: You won't let me stay till he's in the shower, then I won't leave without something personal to remember this moment by.

NICOLE: How about a police record? Is that personal enough for you?

MARCI: Look, there's something on the porch. I'm taking it.

NICOLE: Now you're going to add theft to our list of crimes?

MARCI: *(Slinking off in the direction of the porch)* **Cover me.**

NICOLE: Cover you? What do you mean "cover you"? This isn't Miami Vice, Marci. She is crazy. *(She looks furtively about.)* **Marci, hurry up, I hear another car.**

MARCI: *(Quickly slinking back in, waving her trophy over her head.)* **Look, I got it, I got it.**

NICOLE: What is it?

MARCI: Underwear.

NICOLE: Underwear? You steal a man's underwear? How low can you sink?

MARCI: They're clean.

NICOLE: You don't know that.

MARCI: Yes, I do. He put them on before we went to the beach today.

NICOLE: How do you know?

MARCI: . . . . Never mind.

NICOLE: You watched him get dressed today?

MARCI: No . . . I could see that he had on boxers this morning and when he came out of the house dressed for the beach, he had on these jockeys.

NICOLE: You looked to see what kind of underwear he had on?

MARCI: Don't stand there and tell me you don't.

NICOLE: *(Uncomfortably caught)* **Whatever. I don't want to talk about it. Let's just go.**

MARCI: OK. *(Dancing quietly but happily around the yard)* **I have Jason's underwear, I have Jason's underwear.**

NICOLE: Let me see those. *(She takes them.)* **They're green. He wears teal green underwear.**

MARCI: *(Taking them back)* **They are going to look great nailed to my wall.**

NICOLE: You're sick.

A VOICE FROM OFFSTAGE: Hey, who's out there?

MARCI: Run!! *(And they are gone.)*

TIME TO GO

JANICE: Age 16

KRISSY: Age 21

SETTING: Living room. Janice sits alone on couch. Krissy enters fastening necklace. She looks at Janice, shakes her head, crosses to her and sits on couch next to Janice.

KRISSY: Here, could you help me with these, please? I can't seem to get them fastened.

JANICE: *(Reluctantly moving.)* **Yeah, just lean a little closer so I can get them.**

KRISSY: *(After a moment)* **Janice, are you going to go or what?** *(No response)* **It's almost time to go. I think it would be very rude to be late.**

JANICE: Listen, Krissy, why don't you go on without me? I think I'll just stay here today.

KRISSY: *(Beginning to lose patience)* **We have been through this. You can't stay here. You have to come with me.**

JANICE: I choose not to.

KRISSY: You have no choice.

JANICE: Mom wouldn't mind.

KRISSY: Well, I would.

JANICE: But Mom wouldn't and I think that counts a little more than what you mind and what you don't mind.

KRISSY: *(A different approach)* **Janice, I know this is hard for you to accept, but I really think it will be for the best if you come now.**

JANICE: *(Unmoved)* **I don't.**

KRISSY: I really think that you will be sorry if you don't take this time to say goodbye.

JANICE: I'm not going to say goodbye.

KRISSY: *(Patience wearing thin)* **Then say hello, dammit.**

I don't care, but you have got to go to this funeral.

JANICE: Listen, Mom is dead. I understand that. But she will still be alive in me if I just don't go to this "thing." If you feel it is necessary, then go. I'm not going.

KRISSY: You know, Jani, you have always been like this.

JANICE: Like what?

KRISSY: Just a selfish little brat. You are always so concerned about how you feel. How do you think I feel? You think that this is easy for me? Well, it's not.

JANICE: I know that. *(Blurting it out)* **But I was Mom's favorite and I feel lost . . . I'm sorry. I didn't mean to say that.**

KRISSY: I know. And I also know that you feel lost. *(A pause)* **I also know that you were Mom's favorite. It took a long time for me not to be angry about that.**

JANICE: Angry at me?

KRISSY: At the world. At everyone. That's why this funeral is so hard for me. Harder than it is for you, I think. I was just beginning to be friends with Mom. And now she is gone.

JANICE: Krissy, she's not. She's in our hearts.

KRISSY: Yeah, well, you can't take your heart to lunch and the mall, now can you?

JANICE: Mom was fun to go out with, wasn't she?

KRISSY: I was just beginning to realize that.

JANICE: I am so sorry. I don't think I ever understood the way you two were with each other.

KRISSY: What we were, for the longest time, was at each other's throats. I think we spent more time fighting than we did just talking.

JANICE: I know.

KRISSY: How do you know?

JANICE: I used to listen.

KRISSY: But, you know, it was good fighting. The kind of fighting that lets you grow, even though you tear down something else.

JANICE: Tear down? What do you mean?

KRISSY: Tear down . . . I don't know . . . walls, restraints, fears. I mean, if I hadn't fought with her, if I hadn't broken free of being just the little girl she wanted, I wouldn't be a woman, would I?

JANICE: I guess. I don't know. I know you made Mom cry a lot.

KRISSY: Well, I wasn't exactly tear-free myself.

JANICE: But you loved her?

KRISSY: What a thing to ask. Of course I loved her. And now I am going to say goodbye to her.

JANICE: I just can't.

KRISSY: Why? I don't understand.

JANICE: I'm only 16. I'm not a "woman," I'm a kid. I didn't get that chance to fight, to argue, to tell her I hated her.

KRISSY: Hated her?

JANICE: You know what I mean. Like you. You always said you hated her.

KRISSY: What a terrible thing to remember, especially today. *(Near tears at the memory)* **Why would you bring all that up?**

JANICE: Because you got to say it, to go through it, and get past it. I never will. I will never be able to tell her "I hate you."

KRISSY: It wasn't that great.

JANICE: But you got to. And then you got to say "I love you."

KRISSY: But you always told her that.

JANICE: I think it meant more to her when you said it. It took a lot to say it after the hate.

KRISSY: It wasn't hate. It was anger. Kids say mean things when they are angry. The growing up comes when you can say "I love you."

JANICE: Maybe that's what's wrong. I'm so mad at Mom for dying. So mad that I almost hate her.

KRISSY: Not going to the funeral is not going to bring her back. It's going to look like you didn't love her.

JANICE: But I do. I hate her and I love her, but I am so confused and angry with her for dying. I feel like this is a way to get back at her.

KRISSY: I can almost guarantee you that Mom did not die just to anger you.

JANICE: I know that. But I am angry. So much so that I can't even cry.

KRISSY: You will. Later, it will just hit.

JANICE: I'm so tired.

KRISSY: It's time to go. Everyone is already at the church.

JANICE: Good. With so many people, no one will miss me. I'm not going.

KRISSY: *(Sighing, a long look at JANICE.)* **Fine. I don't want you to feel forced to go. But it's time to go, and I'm going. If you want to ride with me, I'll wait in the car for a couple of minutes. After that, I am leaving.**

JANICE: *(Watching KRISSY, stopping her before she leaves.)* **You knew I was Mom's favorite.**

KRISSY: *(Not bitter, but factual)* **How could I not?**

JANICE: And you still loved her?

KRISSY: *(Small smile, half sad)* **How could I not?** *(She leaves.)*

JANICE: *(A pause while she thinks)* **Dammit.** *(She picks up her purse.)* **Dammit.** *(She heads for the door.)* **Dammit, Mom, I wanted to fight with you, but I never got the chance.** *(As she leaves)* **Dammit.**

GIRLS

HEATHER: Age 16, excited to spread the juicy piece of gossip she has to share, and is loving it.

ANGELA: Also 16, and also happy to join in the cat-fest. Equally loves to dish with the girls.

RACHEL: More intellectual than the other two, but just as pleased to spread the word.

SETTING: Takes place in an eating area at school. It is lunch time. The girls MUST have specific blocking on the eating situation; otherwise, it's just three girls sitting.

HEATHER: Girls, gather 'round. Have I got some wonderful dirt for us all to share.

RACHEL: Oh, tell, tell.

ANGELA: What, who is it about?

RACHEL: Angela, give Heather some room. C'mon, Heath, what's the latest dirt?

HEATHER: Thank you, Rachel. OK. Guess who I saw coming out of Randy's car last night? *(The two girls lean forward intently.)* **Roberta!**

ANGELA: No!

RACHEL: I thought something was going on with those two.

HEATHER: No need to "think" anymore. It is fact.

RACHEL: I can't believe it.

ANGELA: I always suspected them. Does Beth have any idea?

RACHEL: Oh, there's no way.

HEATHER: Well, when she finds out, I do not want to be anywhere in the area.

RACHEL: Talk about a nuclear explosion.

ANGELA: Well, I don't know about you, but if I were Roberta, I would be hiding any pet rabbits I had.

RACHEL: What?

HEATHER and ANGELA: FATAL ATTRACTION! *(The three laugh viciously.)*

RACHEL: Well, I can't say that I blame Randy. The way Beth treats him, I'm surprised he's stuck around this long.

HEATHER: Well, you know why, don't you?

ANGELA: From what I've heard, Randy has every reason NOT to be tense . . . if you get my drift.

RACHEL: C'mon, you don't know that for sure.

HEATHER: Don't be such a naive child, Rachel. A guy like Randy, just look at him.

RACHEL: Well, if it is true, I know Roberta isn't going to be . . . "calming" him, if you get MY drift.

ANGELA: Well . . . .

HEATHER: I am here to tell you, Randy's car windows were pretty steamy, and it wasn't cold out last night.

RACHEL: You don't know that.

HEATHER and ANGELA: OK, Rachel.

HEATHER: Anyway, it will serve her right. Did you see how she behaved at the party last weekend?

ANGELA: It was disgusting. She kept following him around, accusing him of cheating on her.

RACHEL: Well, maybe she had reason.

HEATHER: That's all well and good, but you don't get drunk at a party and pick a fight in front of the entire school. It made her look like a complete fool.

RACHEL: Well, to tell the truth, I never liked the girl. She is always so bitchy to everyone.

ANGELA: Did you see her when she thought Randy was looking at a little freshman girl that was walking by?

HEATHER: I know, she hauled off and hit him.

RACHEL: She's always doing that, just because she knows he won't hit her back.

ANGELA: Maybe that's what she needs, a good hit.

HEATHER: Oh, please. Randy wouldn't ever do that.

And besides, if he did, no matter what the reason, everyone would turn on him like a pit of vicious snakes.

ANGELA: Yeah, you're right.

RACHEL: Well, knowing Roberta, the fight may be on.

HEATHER: What does that mean?

RACHEL: You've seen the girl. I wouldn't mess with her, would you?

ANGELA: Beth wouldn't hit Roberta because Roberta would knock her silly.

HEATHER: Really, Beth is no fool, Rachel. I seriously doubt that Roberta will start anything, but —

RACHEL: She sure wouldn't just stand there and take it.

ANGELA: I know, I . . . ARGH!

HEATHER and RACHEL: What, what's wrong?

ANGELA: ARGH! *(Pointing)* **ARGH!**

HEATHER: Quick, Rachel, grab her. Do you know the Heimlich?

RACHEL: *(Running to grab ANGELA's convulsing body.)* **No, OMIGOD! She's choking!**

ANGELA: Leave me alone, you fools. *(She regains normal speech.)* **Look!** *(The girls look in the direction she is pointing.)*

HEATHER: What? OH NO!

RACHEL: What? OOOHH!

HEATHER: It's Roberta and Randy. Together.

RACHEL: And look, over there. It's Beth.

HEATHER: And they're all walking over this way.

ANGELA: Oh, this is just too good to be true. And we have a front row seat.

RACHEL: Quick, run behind the lockers.

HEATHER: What? Are you crazy? I want to see this.

RACHEL: So do I, but we'll be able to hear if we go over to the lockers and crouch down behind them.

ANGELA: Good thinking, Rachel. Quick, Heather, get

your stuff.

HEATHER: I can't believe this. Won't this look a little obvious?

ANGELA: *(Frantically gathering her things.)* **It will be more obvious if we sit here and listen right under their noses, don't you think?**

RACHEL: For goodness sake, Heather, put some speed on it.

HEATHER: This is ridiculous. I'm not moving. Just because Beth is going to see Roberta and Randy together. What's she going to do, start a fight in the middle of the quad?

RACHEL: Not with us sitting right here watching. That's why we want to give them a little privacy. And that way we can watch it.

ANGELA: Heather, hurry up.

HEATHER: This is stupid.

RACHEL: For someone who couldn't wait to spread the news of the incipient break-up, you're being terribly judgmental.

ANGELA: Uh oh, Heather, Rachel is starting to use those big words. You know what that means, don't you?

HEATHER: OK, OK, I'm coming. Sheesh. *(The girls crouch down behind imaginary lockers.)* **Why do we have to leave just because Beth is going to go into one of her "fits"?**

ANGELA: Because.

HEATHER: Oh, good reason. Stupid me for not seeing it.

RACHEL: Shut up, here they come. Oh, look at Beth's face.

ANGELA: Forget Beth, look at Randy's. The boy is scared to death.

HEATHER: *(Calling out to no one in general.)* **Hide the rabbits!**

ANGELA and RACHEL: *(Pulling her down)* **SHUT UP!**

FRIENDS

SARAH: Nice girl, cares about people's feelings.

JILLIAN: Same, but not quite as patient as Sarah.

DIANE: Wrapped up in boyfriend problems.

SETTING: Scene takes place at Jillian's house by her pool. Jillian and Sarah are the only people on stage.

SARAH: *(Turns over to address JILLIAN.)* **So, Jillian, is Diane coming over or not?**

JILLIAN: I don't know. I invited her, but you know how she's been lately . . . after the break-up!

SARAH: Please, I don't want to hear any more about it. I swear every time we three get together, it is our main topic of conversation.

JILLIAN: You know what is worse? We talk about it even when Diane isn't here. Sarah, we've got to stop this.

SARAH: Really. I mean, what did we talk about before Diane broke up with Matt?

JILLIAN: I think we listened more than talked. We listened to all the reasons Diane should or shouldn't break up with Matt.

SARAH: I'm beginning to wonder if we even have a life worth talking about. *(There is a pause, they look at each other.)* **Maybe we don't.**

JILLIAN: Then don't you think we should get one?

SARAH: How? We spend all of our time trying to make heads or tails of the soap opera that is Diane's life.

JILLIAN: OK. When she gets here, we will try to steer the conversation away from her, and on to other things more interesting.

SARAH: Like us.

JILLIAN: Right! Hey, hand me that suntan lotion. I think I'm starting to burn.

DIANE: *(Entering on JILLIAN's last line.)* **Speaking of burned, guess who called me? Matt. That's why I'm late.**

SARAH: Hi, Di.

JILLIAN: Hi, Di.

DIANE: *(Throwing her towel and stuff on the ground, flopping beside it.)* **I spent 20 minutes on that phone telling him that I didn't want to speak to him ever again.**

JILLIAN: It took you 20 minutes to say "I don't want to talk to you"?

SARAH: Were you speaking in a foreign language?

DIANE: You know how persuasive Matt can be. I held my ground, though. I told him it was over, finished, the end, and I never wanted to see or hear from him again.

JILLIAN: And?

DIANE: Well, I think he is going to come over tonight to try and talk to me. What should I do?

SARAH: *(Looking at JILLIAN)* **Well, I'm going shopping. Jill, what about you?**

JILLIAN: Shopping sounds good.

DIANE: I mean what should I do about Matt?

JILLIAN: Sarah, you want to invite him to go shopping with us?

SARAH: I don't know, might be fun.

DIANE: Hey, I'm serious here. I'm having a problem and I need my friends' advice.

SARAH: Diane, do what you have to do.

DIANE: But I don't know what to do.

JILLIAN: *(Starting to become visibly aggravated)* **Either be there or don't be there.**

SARAH: Really. Make a decision.

DIANE: I don't know. Talk to me. Give me some direction.

JILLIAN: North.

DIANE: What?

JILLIAN: North. It's a direction.

SARAH: Jill. Going a little rough, aren't you?

DIANE: *(Near tears)* **What's wrong with you?**

JILLIAN: Maybe I am going a little rough, but I am getting more than just a little tired of the GREATEST LOVE STORY EVER TOLD.

SARAH: Diane, what Jillian is trying to say, and not very well I might add, is that for the past six months . . .

JILLIAN: I think it's longer.

SARAH: Whatever. Anyway, for the longest time.

JILLIAN: *(Under her breath)* **Looonnnggg.**

SARAH: *(Without stopping but throwing JILLIAN a look.)* **We have been living this . . . this . . .**

JILLIAN: Soap opera.

SARAH: OK, for lack of a better phrase, soap opera, with you, and we have discovered that it is all we ever talk about.

DIANE: What do you mean?

JILLIAN: What we mean is that when you are here, all we talk about is you and Matt. And when you're not here, all we talk about is you and Matt. Do you notice the trend?

DIANE: *(After a pause)* **Well, I'm sorry I came to my so-called friends with my problems. I guess I was under the incorrect belief that that's what friends are for.**

JILLIAN: Thank you, Dionne Warwick.

SARAH: Jillian, please.

DIANE: No, Sarah, let her talk. I'd like to know how she truly feels.

JILLIAN: Fine, Diane. The three of us have been best friends since fourth grade. We have been through quite a few boyfriends since that time, and it has never once affected the friendship we three have

felt for each other . . . Until now.

SARAH: What Jillian is trying to say —

JILLIAN: Sarah, shut up. I know precisely what I'm trying to say and I am more than capable of saying it.

SARAH: I think I will just sit over here and drink my diet coke.

JILLIAN: Do that.

DIANE: Well, Jillian, go on.

JILLIAN: Since you started going out with Matt last February, all we've listened to from you is Matt this and Matt that.

DIANE: It's been a hard relationship.

JILLIAN: You are 16 years old. You are too young to work out a hard relationship.

SARAH: May I cut in here? Diane, we miss you. I don't mean that you go out with Matt too much. We miss YOU. When you are here, Matt is here with you.

DIANE: That's not true. He hardly ever joins us.

JILLIAN: Maybe not physically, but he is here spiritually. You talk about nothing else.

DIANE: But he's on my mind. You know how hard this has been for me to keep together.

SARAH: You are 16 years old with a boyfriend. Not 26 with a husband.

JILLIAN: If the guy is making you this miserable, dump him.

DIANE: I told him today on the phone that I never wanted to see him again.

JILLIAN: And it took you 20 minutes to do that?

SARAH: Don't you see what we mean?

DIANE: Yeah, but don't you see what I mean?

JILLIAN: No, I don't.

DIANE: Well, maybe that is the difference between us. *(She begins to gather her things.)*

SARAH: Where are you going?

DIANE: Home.

JILLIAN: Why?

DIANE: It's obvious I'm not wanted here.

JILLIAN: That's not what we said.

DIANE: *(Leaving)* **Whatever.**

JILLIAN: Fine, whatever.

SARAH: Nice, Jillian, very nice.

JILLIAN: What did I say?

HOMECOMING INTERVIEWS

TERI, DIANE and CILLA: All three are senior girls interviewing for the position of Homecoming Queen, and none of them say out loud what they really think.

SETTING: A bathroom at school. Diane and Teri already in the bathroom, getting ready to be interviewed for Homecoming Queen. There are times when two of the girls will freeze while one speaks her thoughts. The actresses must not show their real feelings during normal conversation. They must maintain friendliness towards each other until the "frozen" period.

TERI: I have never been so nervous in my life.

DIANE: No kidding. Why are we putting ourselves through this?

TERI: I can't believe I am going out there in front of all those people and letting them judge me for Homecoming Queen.

DIANE: I know. This is so stupid.

TERI: You have a really good chance, though.

DIANE: Thanks.

TERI: Do you have your resume?

DIANE: Yeah, want to see it? It's not very good.

TERI: Here, look at mine. There's practically nothing on it.

CILLA: Hi, girls.

TERI and DIANE: Hi Cilla.

CILLA: I think I am going to be sick. You two look great. Diane, I love that dress.

TERI: You did your hair different, didn't you, Cilla? It looks really nice like that.

CILLA: Thanks, I wasn't sure.

DIANE: I may as well not even go out there. You two look great. I look like a pig. I hate this dress.

TERI: Is it new?

DIANE: My mom bought it.

CILLA: It looks nice. It makes you look so slim. *(TERI and CILLA freeze.)*

DIANE: You mean skinny. I know what you mean. Little hypocrite. I hate this lousy dress. I look like a starving bird. I hate Teri. She always has every hair in place. And look at this resume. It's two pages long. She probably made most of it up. *(TERI and CILLA unfreeze.)* **Here's your resume, Teri.**

TERI: Thanks Diane.

CILLA: Do you really think my hair looks good? I wasn't sure. I never know what to do with this hair.

TERI: I know what you mean. Mine always looks like a fur ball the cat just spit up.

DIANE: It looks good, really.

CILLA: Can you believe we are doing this? Who would have thought back in our freshman year that four years later we would be running against each other for Homecoming Queen?

TERI: *(CILLA and DIANE Freeze.)* **Not me, sister. What a tramp. I can't imagine why she's running. What has she done for this school? Probably the football team.** *(CILLA and DIANE unfreeze.)* **No kidding.** *(They all giggle.)*

DIANE: Cilla, can you see if I am wrinkled in the back? This dress is silk and it is just impossible to keep looking fresh.

CILLA: You always have the nicest clothes, Diane.

DIANE: Thank you, Cilia.

TERI: It's true, Diane. I could never carry off some of the things you wear.

CILLA: *(TERI and DIANE Freeze.)* **No kidding, fatso. Where do you get your clothes, anyway? Omar the tentmaker? Didn't I see that little number you have**

on now floating over the last Rams' game with Goodyear printed on the side? *(As TERI and DIANE unfreeze.)* **Move over here in the light, Diane, so I can see it better.**

DIANE: Did you bring your resume?

CILLA: Yes, it's over here in my purse.

TERI: Can I see it?

CILLA: Sure, help yourself. Diane, turn around, you've got a loose thread here.

TERI: *(Looking at CILLA's resume while she and DIANE freeze.)* **What obvious lies.** *(CILLA and DIANE unfreeze.)* **This resume looks really good.**

CILLA: Thanks.

TERI: Diane, can I borrow your lipstick?

DIANE: Sure. *(Hands it to her as TERI and CILLA freeze.)* **Smear it on, honey, you're going to need it.** *(TERI and CILLA unfreeze.)* **That is a great color for you.**

TERI: Thanks.

CILLA: Have you thought about what you're going to say?

TERI: Not yet.

DIANE: Me either. Do they just ask us questions, or what?

CILLA: My sister ran two years ago and she said that they ask you questions like "Why do you think you deserve to be Homecoming Queen?"

DIANE: No way.

TERI: What a dumb question.

CILLA: I know. What do they think we're going to say? "Because I'm the best girl in this school?"

ALL THREE: *(Face front and say at the same time.)* **Damn right I am.**

DIANE: No kidding. What a stupid question.

TERI: Leave it to football players.

CILLA: *(Looking in the mirror)* **I should have done my**

hair the way I normally do it. *(CILLA and DIANE freeze.)*

TERI: No, I think washing it was a good idea. *(As they unfreeze.)* **Cilla, calm down, it looks fine.**

CILLA: *(TERI and DIANE freeze.)* **How can you tell? Where are your glasses today, four eyes?** *(As they unfreeze.)* **Thanks. I am so nervous.**

DIANE: We all are.

TERI: I was so nervous, I left my glasses at home. I'll be lucky if I don't walk onto the stage and keep walking right off of it. *(TERI and CILLA freeze.)*

DIANE: If you fell on your face, it could only be an improvement. *(As they unfreeze.)* **Just hang on to me, I'll help you.**

TERI: You are such a good friend.

CILLA: Just think, four short years ago, we were standing in this bathroom, three scared little freshmen.

DIANE: Hiding from the senior girls.

TERI: They all seemed so grown-up and mature.

CILLA: Now it's us.

TERI: We're the grown-up mature ones now.

DIANE: Running for Homecoming Queen.

CILLA: Who would have thought? We've come a long way in four years.

DIANE: And we are still friends.

TERI: Not a lot of girls at this school can say that.

CILLA: *(Looking at her watch.)* **It's time to go in.** *(They all hold hands and look at each other in the mirror, and take a deep breath.)*

ALL THREE: Good luck. *(They turn, walk Up-stage three steps, turn back around and say their thoughts out loud.)* **You're gonna need it.**

TELEPHONES

ANNA, BETH, CARY and DINA: All teenage girls.

SETTING: Each character is in her own space, and does not physically relate to the others in the scene. They all relate to each other as they speak on the phone, but they cannot ***see*** each other. All four girls come onto their playing area at the same time. It must be established that they are in their own space. ***The phone rings.***

ANNA: Hello?

BETH: *(Very upset)* **Anna? Is that you?**

ANNA: Yes. Who is this?

BETH: It's me, Beth.

ANNA: Omigod, what's wrong with you?

CARY: *(Dials during above dialogue.)* **C'mon, pick up the phone.**

DINA: *(Reaching for her phone)* **Hello?**

CARY: I am so angry.

DINA: Cary? What?

CARY: Dina, you are not going to believe what just happened.

BETH: Gary and I broke up.

CARY: Gary and Beth just broke up.

DINA and ANNA: *(Each with her own emotion)* **No way!**

BETH and CARY: *(Each with her own emotion)* **I knew this would happen. I just knew it.**

BETH: I walked into the library, and there they were, heads close together.

ANNA: The tramp.

DINA: What did you do when she saw you?

CARY: Nothing, what could I do? I just looked at her.

BETH: Anna, you should have seen her. She gave me the most dirty look.

ANNA: She is such a bitch.

DINA: She is such a wimp.

BETH and CARY: No kidding.

ANNA and DINA: I can't stand her sometimes.

CARY: Anyway, all Gary and I were doing was studying. I can't help it if my shoulder just happened to be touching his.

BETH: You should have seen her, rubbing up against him.

ANNA and DINA: What did Gary do?

CARY and BETH: That's the best part, wait till I tell you.

BETH: He just sat there and looked so guilty.

ANNA: You mean he just looked at you? He didn't say anything?

CARY: Yeah, he just sat there.

DINA: What did you do?

BETH: Then that tramp flicks back her hair like she always does.

CARY: *(Flicking her hair)* **Well . . .**

ANNA: I can't *stand* when she does that.

CARY: I just bit my pencil so I would keep my mouth shut.

BETH: Then she sticks the pencil in her mouth and practically licks it, if you know what I mean.

ANNA and DINA: I know what you mean.

BETH: So I just turned around and walked away.

ANNA: Just like that?

CARY: And then just like that she walks away. Who does she think she is?

ANNA: Who does she think she is?

DINA and BETH: Who knows?

CARY: Dina, hold on, I've got a call.

DINA: Just call me back, I've got some stuff to do, OK?

CARY: Sure. But don't go away, there's more.

DINA: Don't worry. *(She hangs up and dials a number.)*

BETH: I'm calling Gary right now. I'll call you right back.

ANNA: OK. *(Hangs up.)*

CARY: Hello? Oh. Hi Gary.

BETH: Jeez, why doesn't he get call waiting. *(She dials again.)*

ANNA: Hello?

DINA: Did you hear?

ANNA: Hear what?

CARY: No, I haven't talked to Beth since the library. Why?

DINA: Beth and Gary broke up.

ANNA: I heard.

CARY: She said what?

DINA: Who told you?

ANNA: Beth.

BETH: Who is he talking to? *(She dials another number.)*

CARY: Gary, of course you can come over to talk.

ANNA: Dina, just a second, I've got a call.

DINA: OK, but come right back.

ANNA: Hello?

BETH: It's busy.

CARY: Well, I'm upset too. Beth is one of my best friends.

ANNA: Beth, I've got Dina on the other line. How does she know about you and Gary?

CARY: In about an hour? Fine.

BETH: Put her on the conference.

ANNA: Are you still there?

DINA: Yeah, who was on the line?

BETH: It's me.

DINA: Oh, I'm so sorry.

CARY: I'm sure it will all work out.

BETH: How do you know?

DINA: Cary told me.

ANNA: I'm sure she had quite a lot to say.

CARY: In an hour, then. See ya. *(She dials.)*

DINA: Not really. She said that they were just studying.

BETH: **Yeah, each other.**

ANNA: **You know what a mantrap that girl is.**

DINA: **Well . . . Oh, wait, I've got a call.**

BETH: **I bet it's her.**

ANNA: **Call me back later, OK?**

DINA: **Sure.** *(She clicks.)* **Hello?**

CARY: **Guess who's coming over in an hour?**

ANNA: **I'm sure Cary is sitting by the phone right now waiting for you to call.**

BETH and DINA: *(Each with their own emotion)* **No way!**

DINA and ANNA: **Well, what are you going to do?**

BETH: **Well, I'm not going to just sit here and wait for him.**

CARY: **Just sit right here and wait for him.**

ANNA: **Hey, c'mon over here for a while.**

DINA: **Well, you call me the minute he leaves, OK?**

CARY: **For sure.** *(Hangs up, straightens herself up for GARY.)*

DINA: *(Dialing)* **Oh, please be there.**

BETH: **Anna, hang on, maybe it's him.**

ANNA: **Well, come over and tell me.**

BETH: **Hello?**

DINA: **Hi. Are you OK?**

BETH: **I guess.**

CARY: **Mom?**

MOM: *(Off-stage)* **Yes?**

CARY: **I'm going out for a little while with Gary, OK?**

MOM: **Not too long, it's a school night.** *(CARY rolls her eyes and continues to get ready.)*

DINA: **Tell me everything.**

BETH: **What's there to tell? Gary obviously wants that little tramp, Cary.**

ANNA: **Mom?**

MOM: **What?**

ANNA: **Beth's coming over for a little while, OK?**

MOM: Not too long, it's a school night. *(ANNA rolls her eyes and dials the phone.)*

DINA: What are you going to do?

BETH: Heck, I don't know.

CARY: Hello?

ANNA: Hi, so tell me everything.

DINA: I think you should call him.

BETH: I tried. His line was busy.

DINA: Oh?

CARY: What's to tell?

ANNA: What do you think, I'm stupid? You've been scheming on Gary for a long time.

BETH: I don't know what I should do.

ANNA and DINA: You know what I think?

CARY and BETH: What?

ANNA and DINA: I think he's a jerk.

CARY and BETH: I know. But he's so cute.

MOM: Are you still on the phone?

ALL FOUR GIRLS: *(Whiny teenage girl voice)* **MOTHER!**

MOM: Now, dear. Get off now.

BETH: I've gotta go.

DINA: Me, too.

ANNA: My mom's calling me.

CARY: Mine, too.

ANNA and DINA: Call me later and we'll talk.

BETH and CARY: *(Each with her own feeling)* **Maybe.**

ALL FOUR: Bye. *(Hang up, take 10 seconds in their own room to do whatever they would do.)*

MOM: Honey, come here, please. *(Each reacts her own way according to whatever hidden agenda she has.)*

EACH: Coming.

STUDY HOUR

MEG, JO, and DI: All seniors, all attractive, intelligent, teenage girls.

SETTING: Jo's bedroom, strewn with papers, books, empty diet coke cans, etc. The girls are studying, or at least trying to.

MEG: *(Throwing papers up in absolute defeat)* **I've lost all sense of concentration. I can do no more.**

DI: I know what you mean. I can't think anymore. I've thought all I can think.

JO: Meg, Di, c'mon. We've got to finish this assignment or we are going to be joining the ranks of the five-year high school student.

MEG: Lighten up, Jo. It's one lousy class.

JO: Well, this one lousy class is the one we need to graduate.

DI: Isn't this the stupidest thing you ever heard of? You can have a complete 3.0 GPA and screw up this one class of Econ in your last semester of your senior year, and you are dust.

JO: Be that as it may. Do it we must, and do it we will . . .

MEG: Yes, oh mighty leader. *(A few moments of silence while they study. Then MEG looks up from her book.)* **Di, did you see Eric today?**

DI: Please, don't remind me. Gorgeous or what?

MEG: He must have his 501s custom fit. No one has that good a body.

JO: Study, girls, let's keep our minds where they should be.

MEG: Are you going to sit there and tell me you can study when Eric McNally's name has been mentioned?

JO: Yes. Define GNP.

DI: GNP. Oh, I know. Great New Pants.

MEG: Yes! *(MEG and DI high five.)*

JO: Ladies!

DI: C'mon, loosen up. You can't tell me you wouldn't drop this book in two seconds flat if Eric called you now?

JO: No, I wouldn't . . . *(Giggling)* **It would take me at least three seconds.**

MEG: *(Singsong, tosses books aside.)* **Break time.**

JO: I'll get the food.

DI: I have diet cokes, the better to wash down chips and dips!

MEG: Did you see Greta today? I swear, she practically threw herself at Eric's feet.

DI: I can think of much better places at which to throw myself at Eric.

JO: *(To MEG, referring jokingly about DI.)* **And yes, she is a tramp.**

MEG: No, really. Greta may as well tattoo "for sale" on her forehead the way she throws herself at all the guys.

DI: Her and her cute big blue eyes and blond hair. That ever-so-helpless look she gives them.

MEG: You'd think that guys today would see through that simpering stupid attitude.

JO: *(Imitating Greta)* **Oh, please, Eric. I just don't understand this math problem. Two plus two. That's five, right?**

DI: The sickening part of the whole thing is that if we tried it, the guys would look at us as if we lost our minds.

JO: What does she have that we don't have? Why can she get away with that stupidity, and we can't?

MEG: Because intelligence shines like a beacon through our eyes. The men know when we put on an act. With her, it's no act.

DI: **You can't mean that you think that she is really that dumb?**

MEG: **It's the only thing I can come up with. No one is that good an actress.**

JO: **Meg has made a very good point.**

DI: **It's impossible . . . no one can be that stupid. Watch, I can do it.**

JO: **What do you mean?**

DI: **Wait. Let's think about her. First her looks.**

MEG: **Easy. Dumb.**

DI: **C'mon. Give me more than that.**

JO: **I get it. OK. First. Ummm.**

DI: **Basics. Her hair.**

MEG: **Blond. Blonder than blond.**

JO: **No, no, no! I know a lot of really smart blonds.**

MEG: **Oh, I know. The style.**

DI: **Yeah. Fruffed out. Wait, let me get my brush and spray.**

JO: **Are you going to do this?**

DI: **What the heck, give it a shot just to see if I can.**

MEG: **Go for it.** *(Attacks DI's hair with spray and brush.)*

JO: **Oooh, let me help.** *(They proceed to fruff out DI's hair and ad lib comments.)* **Yes, yes, yes!**

MEG: **What else?**

DI: **Think. What else is it?**

MEG: **I know. It's the way she looks at the guys. Even if they are shorter than she is, she looks up at them.**

JO: **What?**

MEG: **Like this.** *(Demonstrates by bending head down and raising eyes up, so it appears that she is looking through eyelashes.)*

DI: **Omigod. That is absolutely ridiculous.**

JO: **But it's her. It's her. Try it.**

DI: **Geez.**

MEG: **Yeah! That's it.**

DI: How does she do this all day? It hurts my neck.

JO: The smile. I know how she does the smile. I read it somewhere. A play I think. She just drops her mouth and opens her eyes very wide. See, it's vacuous, but you don't wrinkle. *(Demonstrates)*

DI: *(Trying the simpering smile, fluttering her eyelashes.)* **Hi, Eric.**

MEG: *(Making her fingers an X sign)* **ARGH! It's the Woman of the Living Stupid!**

DI: *(Still being simpering)* **Meggie, I don't get it.**

JO: That's not what we hear.

MEG and DI: OOOHHH!!!

MEG: Now the walk. The walk is very special.

JO: How does it look?

DI: I don't need any help on this one. Watch. I've been studying it for years. *(She takes tiny little steps, knees very close together.)* **See, it's these itty bitty little steps. I remember watching this when we were in P.E. together in 7th grade. This walk looks ridiculous on the basketball court, but in the Quad in a mini-skirt, the guys love it.**

MEG: OK, now do the whole thing. You be Greta, I'll be Eric.

JO: And I'll be sick.

DI: *(The whole look put together.)* **Hi, Eric.** *(Eyelashes aflutter)*

MEG: What's goin' on? How'd you do on that math test?

DI: Oh Eric. You know how silly I am about math. I just can't think so hard. *(Back to self.)* **I think I'm going to be sick.**

JO: But you've got it. I think she's got it.

MEG: Thank you Henry Higgins. Di, how does it feel?

DI: How does it look?

MEG: Pretty stupid.

JO: But if it works . . .

DI: *(Brushing out hair)* **Do you really want to get a guy if**

he is the kind that would fall for that?

MEG: Would you really lower yourself to that level?

DI: Would you desert your moral principles?

MEG: Compromise your ideals?

JO: For Eric? You mean for gorgeous, tall, sweet, breathtaking divine Eric? In a flash.

MEG: Without a second thought.

DI: No problem.

JO: Let's do it.

MEG: Now?

JO: Got a brush?

DI: Use mine. I'll teach you the walk, too.

MEG: This is really stupid.

JO: I know. But it's a lot more interesting than Econ.

BOYS

THE DANCE . . . 2

JOHN: Seventeen, feeling some misgivings about going to the dance with Mary because she is treating him strangely.

AL: John's best friend, more worldly wise to the ways of women, sees it as his job to guide his innocent friend.

AL: John, I'm going to reserve the limo for Homecoming and I need your money by Friday.

JOHN: You might have to wait a little longer.

AL: I can't. The guy says that if I don't have the money there by Friday, we will lose the limo. Wait till you see it, it's great.

JOHN: Al, I might not be going to Homecoming.

AL: I thought Mary said that she would go.

JOHN: She did. But now . . . I don't know.

AL: What happened?

JOHN: She called me last night and said that she wanted to make sure that I knew that we were going as "just friends."

AL: Oooh.

JOHN: Really. "Just friends." I mean, what else did she think? I can't believe it.

AL: So, what did you say?

JOHN: I said, yes, of course I knew that. God, she acted like she was doing me a favor.

AL: Did you tell her that?

JOHN: No, I just told her that friends was all I wanted to go as in the first place. She has been acting so weird since I asked her to go.

AL: Well, John, I'm not surprised. I told you not to make a big deal out of asking her. But no, you had to go all out and get a stupid balloon and those dumb flowers. You couldn't just say, "Hey, Mary, want to go to Homecoming?"

JOHN: I wanted it to be special. I thought she would like it.

AL: You were obviously wrong. Why do you always do that?

JOHN: Do what?

AL: Go overboard on everything. You have to make a big deal and then you always end up getting used for a doormat. You don't see that happening to me.

JOHN: Doormat. Thanks.

AL: Oh, c'mon. It's not that bad. So, now you know and she knows you are going as friends, so everything's cool.

JOHN: I guess so.

AL: Now what's wrong?

JOHN: I didn't tell you everything.

AL: What? She wants you to wear brown.

JOHN: Don't be stupid. You know, she's been acting kind of funny ever since I asked her to this dance. She avoids me at school, doesn't talk to me in class anymore. It's weird.

AL: Why is she doing that? Did you ask her?

JOHN: Yes. She said she wasn't. But she acted really funny about it.

AL: What do you mean?

JOHN: I asked her flat out why she was doing that, and she said I was imagining things.

AL: I don't understand this at all. Weren't you two like the best of friends not more than a week ago?

JOHN: That's what I thought. And then I asked her to this stupid dance and it's been horrible ever since.

AL: Have you guys stopped talking on the phone?

JOHN: Oh, that's the best part. I asked her if she wanted me to not talk to her at school, and we could just talk at night on the phone. She said . . . are you ready? She said, YES! She doesn't want me to talk

to her at school. She just wants to talk to me at night on the phone.

AL: You can't be serious.

JOHN: Yes I can. Can you believe it?

AL: I can't believe you are seriously thinking of still seeing her.

JOHN: What?

AL: You can't still be thinking of taking her to Homecoming, can you?

JOHN: Well, I . . . uh . . .

AL: Omigod! You are an idiot.

JOHN: Why?

AL: The girl avoids you at school, tells you that you two are going as "just friends," and then has the nerve to tell you that you aren't ALLOWED to talk to her at school? Only at night on the phone? And you are still going to spend $500 on Homecoming for her? YOU ARE AN IDIOT!!

JOHN: Al, you make it sound much worse than it is.

AL: John, she won't allow you to talk to her in front of her friends at school. It doesn't get much worse than that.

JOHN: *(Thinking a moment)* **Yeah, you're right.**

AL: You're darn right, I'm right. You get on that phone right now and tell that wench that you aren't going to that dance with her.

JOHN: But it's only a week before the dance. Who will she go with if I don't go with her?

AL: What an IDIOT! Don't be such a wimp. Let it be her problem.

JOHN: She already got a dress.

AL: Let her wear it when she talks to her friends at school. Of course, you'll never see it, because you're not ALLOWED to talk to her at school. Call her, John.

JOHN: Now?

AL: Yes, now. If you wait till you get home, you'll wimp out. I know how you are.

JOHN: Yeah, maybe you're right.

AL: *(Picking up the phone and dialing)* **Here.**

JOHN: It's ringing...she's probably not home... Oh, Hi, Mary? Yeah, this is John. Listen. I...uh... what? Red?

AL: What's she saying?

JOHN: *(Putting hand over the phone to talk to AL and still listening to MARY)* **She's telling me what color corsage to get.**

AL: Tell her, John.

JOHN: Mary, I . . . Huh? Oh, I don't know. Well, yeah, I guess we could do that.

AL: What, what?

JOHN: Hold on a second, Mary. *(To AL)* **She wants to know if it would be all right if we could stop at her grandma's before we head out so she could see Mary in her formal.** *(Back to MARY)*

AL: I don't believe this. Tell her!!

JOHN: Huh? Oh, Al. I'm at his house . . . . Mary says hi.

AL: Yeah, but will she say hi at school?

JOHN: Shut up . . . No, not you, Mary. Al. Anyway, the reason I called was . . . Oh, really? *(To AL)* **She got her dress from the dressmaker's today.** *(To MARY)* **Oh, yeah, I can't wait . . . No kidding, She is?**

AL: John . . . . You better tell her before it's too late.

JOHN: Yeah, well, I'll call you tonight.

AL: I'm dying here.

JOHN: OK, bye. *(He hangs up.)* **I didn't tell her.**

AL: Oh, really? What a wimp.

JOHN: Al, her sister is flying in from college to see her off to her first formal. What was I supposed to do?

AL: What a wimp.

JOHN: I know. I'm trapped.

AL: Like a rat.

JOHN: So, it's one night out of my life.

AL: And $500. For a girl who won't talk to you at school.

JOHN: I bet this is one of those things that in the years to come I will look back and laugh at.

AL and JOHN: Nah.

THE PARTY

BRIAN: At sixteen, he is awakening the morning after a party at his home the weekend his parents have left him on his own.

ROBERT: Brian's best friend, also awakening from the night's festivities.

SETTING: The scene opens with Brian slowly awakening, looking around at what was once a lovely family room, now the scene of nuclear holocaust, otherwise known as the morning after a party. Also, each "Oh my God" is said with a different feeling to convey the subtext of the moment.

BRIAN: *(Slowly, and in disbelief)* **Oh my god.** *(He gets up, looks around, afraid to touch anything.)* **Oh my god.**

ROBERT: *(Entering, rubbing his eyes)* **Oh my god.** *(He looks at BRIAN.)* **Oh my god.**

BRIAN: Can you believe this?

ROBERT: Oh my god.

BRIAN: What time is it?

ROBERT: *(Squinting at his watch)* **About 10:30.**

BRIAN: Morning or night?

ROBERT: *(Moving a curtain aside and looking out.)* **The sun's out so it must be morning.**

BRIAN: So that means my parents will be home soon. *(He surveys the damage again.)* **Oh my god.**

ROBERT: Busted.

BRIAN: Where is everybody?

ROBERT: The party ended about 3:30. Do you have any Pepsi?

BRIAN: Why?

ROBERT: To clear away the fuzz on my teeth.

BRIAN: Yeah, in the ice chest over here.

ROBERT: Thanks. *(He crosses towards BRIAN.)* **What the**

heck is that?

BRIAN: What?

ROBERT: In your ear?

BRIAN: What? *(He goes to a mirror.)* **Oh my god.**

ROBERT: It's an earring.

BRIAN: Where did that come from?

ROBERT: You didn't have it yesterday, did you?

BRIAN: No. *(He looks at Robert.)* **Did you?**

ROBERT: What?

BRIAN: Have an earring.

ROBERT: Heck no, my dad would kill me.

BRIAN: Then be prepared to die. Look.

ROBERT: *(He sees the earring in his ear.)* **Oh my god.**

BRIAN: Tracy.

ROBERT: What?

BRIAN: Tracy. That's what she meant when she said "I want Brian." I thought she meant she "wanted" me.

ROBERT: So that's what Kristie meant about "I'll take Robert." Oh my god.

BRIAN: *(Touching his ear.)* **This hurts a little bit, you know?**

ROBERT: Don't be a wimp, babies get this done all the time, not to mention girls. *(He touches his ear.)* **Ow!**

BRIAN: Lord have mercy.

ROBERT: Look at this place.

BRIAN: It's 10:30 now? That means my parents will be home in about three hours. Three hours to turn this back into a house.

ROBERT: *(Looking around)* **You're a dead man.**

BRIAN: You gonna help me?

ROBERT: Where do we start?

BRIAN: *(As they begin to clean.)* **Anywhere.**

ROBERT: Your parents are going to kill you. I told you not to have a party here.

BRIAN: Was that before or after you made up the flyers?

ROBERT: What flyers?

BRIAN: The ones that everyone had in their hot little hands announcing time and place.

ROBERT: Oh. That flyer.

BRIAN: Yes, that flyer.

ROBERT: Good party, though, huh?

BRIAN: From the looks of this place, a great one.

ROBERT: Did you catch Pat?

BRIAN: Catch him what?

ROBERT: Charging admission.

BRIAN: Did we charge admission?

ROBERT: No, but Pat was collecting from people before he would let them in.

BRIAN: No way. How much did he get?

ROBERT: I think he said he got about $50.

BRIAN: Did he leave any of it?

ROBERT: Yeah, right. Pat leave money?

BRIAN: Sorry, I'm in a daze.

ROBERT: Should I take a look upstairs?

BRIAN: Did anyone go upstairs? I told everyone to stay down here.

ROBERT: You also told them not to use the phone. Mark was calling Lisa.

BRIAN: Lisa. You mean Lisa who is in New York?

ROBERT: Yes, Lisa who is in New York.

BRIAN: I am a dead man.

ROBERT: I told him to get off the phone. He said you said it was OK.

BRIAN: I thought he said he was calling for a pizza. No wonder Domino's never showed up.

ROBERT: So, should I look upstairs or not?

BRIAN: Yeah, let's take a look. It's starting to look a little less like hell down here.

ROBERT: Why don't I go, and report to you? That way I can start up there and you can finish down here.

BRIAN: OK, good idea.

ROBERT: *(ROBERT heads upstairs, stops and speaks.)* **You know, it was a great party. Did you see Trish?**

BRIAN: Yes, Robert, I saw Trish.

ROBERT: She looked great, didn't she?

BRIAN: I guess so. Robert, let's not start on Trish and how beautiful she is. I have heard it all before and it is getting a little old.

ROBERT: Someday, Bri, I am going to ask her out.

BRIAN: Yes, and some day, I will be playing for the Washington Senator Baseball team.

ROBERT: There is no Washington Senator team.

BRIAN: I think you grasp my point. Now, check upstairs.

ROBERT: Fine. *(He heads upstairs.)* **Thanks for your emotional support.**

BRIAN: Yeah, yeah. *(He looks around.)* **Oh my god.**

ROBERT: *(From upstairs)* **Oh my god.**

BRIAN: What? *(He heads for the stairs.)*

ROBERT: You don't want to know.

BRIAN: *(Off stage)* **Oh my god.**

WHAT ARE YOU GONNA DO?

FRANK: Seventeen with a fairly callous attitude towards women and their needs.

MIKE: Also seventeen, however a bit more mature in his outlook towards life. Sensitive to feelings of others.

RICK: A good friend of the two, troubled by this new adult complication in his life.

SETTING: The scene takes place in a locker room as Rick, Mike, and Frank are getting ready for school after morning practice. It will be the director's decision in the blocking and character definition as to what they were practicing. Frank and Rick are already on the scene. Mike is Offstage.

FRANK: Rick, hand me that shoe.

RICK: *(Tossing it to him)* **Catch.**

FRANK: You going out with Kristina tonight?

RICK: Probably.

FRANK: You've been seeing a lot of her lately.

RICK: Not as much as I'd like. *(They laugh.)* **I swear, the only word that girl says lately is "No." Sometimes I ask her if she wants something I know she likes, like candy, just to hear a "yes" out of her.**

FRANK: Dump her.

RICK: That's what I've always liked about you. You're a very sensitive guy.

FRANK: That's what I'm always saying to the girls. "Hey, wench, I'm sensitive."

RICK: That's why you're a popular guy.

FRANK: I have my ways.

RICK: Speaking of ways, stay out of Mike's today.

FRANK: No kidding. What was with him this morning? He's hardly said two words.

RICK: He said three to me. I asked him if he and Lara

wanted to come with me and Kristina tonight and he said "Go to hell."

FRANK: Maybe they broke up.

RICK: Maybe.

MIKE: *(Entering on the last exchange)* **No, we didn't break up. But, maybe we should have about three months ago.**

RICK: Why three months ago?

MIKE: Because then I wouldn't be in the mess I'm in now. Lara's pregnant.

RICK: No way. Is she sure?

MIKE: Pretty sure. We'll know for certain this afternoon.

FRANK: Is it yours?

RICK: Frank!

MIKE: What a jerk.

FRANK: You never know. Didn't you guys break up for a few days a couple of months ago?

MIKE: Yes, but that doesn't mean she was with somebody else.

FRANK: Like I said, "You never know."

MIKE: That's true, but . . .

RICK: Mike, come on. You know Lara better than that. You were the one who broke up with her. She was torn up.

FRANK: So, maybe she found comfort in the arms of someone else for one night.

MIKE: Stop it, Frank.

FRANK: Just posing a theory.

MIKE: Just shut up.

RICK: *(After a moment's quiet.)* **So, what are you gonna do?**

MIKE: I don't know.

FRANK: Dump her.

RICK: Frank! Shut up.

MIKE: I can't do that.

FRANK: Unless she can prove it's yours, you don't have a problem.

MIKE: I can't believe you're saying this.

RICK: I can. Just shut up, OK Frank?

FRANK: Just trying to help out.

MIKE: We talked about options. I just don't know.

FRANK: Abortion?

MIKE: God, I hate that word.

FRANK: You said you were looking for options.

MIKE: I know. It's just an ugly word.

RICK: What about adoption?

MIKE: Yeah, we talked about that, too.

FRANK: She'd have to go away.

MIKE: Why?

FRANK: It'd be hard for her to hold her head up in this town being pregnant at sixteen.

RICK: That's not really fair to her, then is it?

FRANK: She's the one who got in trouble.

MIKE: Well, I was right there with her.

FRANK: So she says.

MIKE: One more crack like that and you're dead.

FRANK: I'm just saying what everybody else will say.

RICK: So, she's a tramp?

FRANK: Look at Kristina. She says "no". Look at every girl I've gone out with, they all say "no," too.

RICK: *(Sarcastically)* I wonder why?

MIKE: We could get married.

RICK and FRANK: NO!

MIKE: Why not? It would be paying for this mistake in the only right way.

RICK: Marriage is hard enough without it being a "payment for a mistake." Look at Frank's parents.

FRANK: Really, they can't stand each other. The divorce was messy, but now that it's over, as long as they leave me alone, I'm fine.

RICK: **So,** *(Pointing to FRANK)* **is this what you want for your child?**

MIKE: I don't know. I just don't know.

RICK: Have you told your parents?

MIKE: No way. Not until I know for sure. Even then, depending on what Lara decides, I don't know if I'll tell them.

FRANK: What do you mean, "what Lara decides"?

MIKE: It's her decision. I told her I will do whatever she thinks is best.

RICK: Isn't that kind of throwing the whole thing onto her shoulders?

FRANK: Hey, it's her problem.

MIKE: It's our problem. But she is the one that has to live with the decision.

FRANK: I vote for abortion.

MIKE: I didn't put it up for a vote.

FRANK: I still vote for abortion.

RICK: I don't know. That's so . . . I don't know. I just don't like it.

FRANK: Mike, do you want that girl to be pregnant?

MIKE: That's stupid. Of course I don't.

FRANK: Does she want to be pregnant?

MIKE: Of course not. She's a wreck.

FRANK: Then, it's abortion. That way, everybody is happy.

RICK: Except the kid.

FRANK: Rick, don't start with your preaching about the rights of the unborn.

RICK: But, don't they have rights?

FRANK: Not when they interfere with the rights of the sixteen-year-old parents who have no business having a kid.

RICK: But there's adoption.

FRANK: Oh, fine. So that means Lara gives up almost

a whole year of her life, to give a kid away to someone she doesn't even know? And I'll tell you something else, I read that 75 percent of teen mothers end up keeping the kid. *(To MIKE)* **Is that what you want . . . Daddy?**

MIKE: *(More upset with each phrase.)* **I don't know. I don't know. I don't know.**

FRANK: Well, you better find out. Do what's right for you.

RICK: Do what's right for everybody.

MIKE: I'm only sixteen. I shouldn't have to make this kind of decision about my life. *(They are all quiet for a moment.)*

FRANK: It's almost time for class. We better get going.

MIKE: I'm not going. I'm gonna find Lara. We need to talk. We've got to figure something out.

RICK: When does she find out for sure?

MIKE: She's got a 3:00 appointment today at the clinic.

FRANK: Are you taking her?

MIKE: Yeah. Her parents don't know, either.

RICK: We'll be at my house. Call us and let us know, OK?

MIKE: Yeah. I am so confused.

RICK: Think how Lara feels. It's her body, you know.

MIKE: But, it's our life.

RICK: In more ways than one.

MIKE: Yeah.

FRANK: Call us. You know if you need anything, we're there.

MIKE: Yeah. Thanks. *(He leaves.)*

FRANK: Damn.

RICK: No kidding. I'm gonna find Kristina and give her such a hug. "No" sounds really good right now.

FRANK: Really.

RICK: See you.

FRANK: Yeah. *(They look at each other.)* **Damn.**

DATING

KEVIN: Experiencing love for the first time.

DANNY: His best friend.

SETTING: Takes place on a Friday, late afternoon, Kevin's house.

KEVIN: *(Singing that old Motown song)* **Love, love, love, makes me do foolish things. Hmmm mmmm.** *(etc.)*

DANNY: *(Entering, listening for a moment)* **Don't give up your day job.**

KEVIN: *(A bit embarrassed)* **Hey, Danny. I didn't see you. How are you doing?**

DANNY: I hope I feel better than you sound.

KEVIN: Hey, I'm a man in love.

DANNY: Yeah, well. Getting a little dressed up for tonight, aren't you?

KEVIN: Well, I'm thinking of asking Michelle to go steady. You know, a sort of permanent thing.

DANNY: And you have to dress up tonight for that?

KEVIN: I like to look good for her.

DANNY: Wait a minute. You mean she's coming with us?

KEVIN: Us?

DANNY: Yes, us. Kevin, I got these tickets to the game for us a month ago. I only have two. One for you and one for me.

KEVIN: Oh my god, is that tonight?

DANNY: You are not telling me you forgot?

KEVIN: I guess I am. I'm really sorry.

DANNY: Can't you just call her and cancel?

KEVIN: No. I can't do that to her.

DANNY: But you can cancel on me?

KEVIN: You're a guy. It's different.

DANNY: I thought I was your best friend.

KEVIN: You are. That's why I know you'll understand.

DANNY: Surprise, I don't understand.

KEVIN: Chill out, Danny.

DANNY: You chill out, Kevin. I paid for these tickets, we made these plans a month ago. What's the deal here?

KEVIN: We made those plans before I met Michelle.

DANNY: Oh, that's right. Miss America, Albert Schweitzer, Blaze Starr, and Kermit the Frog all wrapped up in one tight little blond package.

KEVIN: Hey, that's enough, Danny.

DANNY: That's not even close to enough. You have become abnormally controlled by this girl.

KEVIN: She doesn't control me.

DANNY: Then why can't you go?

KEVIN: It's not that I can't. I don't want to.

DANNY: Thanks a lot.

KEVIN: Grow up, Danny. You of all people should understand.

DANNY: And what does that mean?

KEVIN: How many times have you cancelled out on me because of Susan?

DANNY: That was a while ago, so don't bring up the past.

KEVIN: You're telling me that if Susan called you right now, you wouldn't drop these plans in a hot New York minute?

DANNY: I wouldn't.

KEVIN: Yeah, right.

DANNY: I wouldn't. Susan and I have a much more mature relationship than you do with Michelle.

KEVIN: Maybe that's because you two have been going out for a year now and it's old. Michelle and I have been seeing each other for only a month. It's new and I don't intend to screw it up.

DANNY: In other words, you're whipped.

KEVIN: Hey! I did not ever talk that way about you and Michelle. God knows I had plenty of reason and opportunity, but I didn't.

DANNY: What do you mean, "reason and opportunity"?

KEVIN: Nothing, forget it.

DANNY: You have something to say, buddy, say it.

KEVIN: Why bother. It's in the past, let it stay there.

DANNY: No way. You talk to me. What "reason and opportunity"?

KEVIN: Fine, you want to talk about it, we'll talk about it.

DANNY: OK, what?

KEVIN: For example, the TGIO dance on the last day of school last year.

DANNY: What about it?

KEVIN: It was our last party thing as juniors, and we had made plans in our FRESHMAN year to party hard. Do you remember those plans?

DANNY: Vaguely.

KEVIN: Vaguely, right. *(He shakes his head in annoyance.)* **So, we had these plans. Our last great time to do something fun in high school without it affecting our college acceptances. And what did we do?**

DANNY: I don't remember.

KEVIN: You're right. You don't remember. Because there was nothing TO remember. You drove, we picked up Susan, we got to the dance, you and Susan stayed in various dark corners all night long, and then you two left. I had to get a ride with Steve.

DANNY: You were supposed to be with Erin.

KEVIN: I can't stand that girl. You know it now, you knew it then. You were just too wrapped up in Susan to even notice that I wasn't in the car when you left.

DANNY: Grow up, Kevin.

KEVIN: I have. So I, and my grown up self are seeing

Michelle tonight.

DANNY: So, what am I supposed to do?

KEVIN: Take Susan to the game.

DANNY: Oh, great fun. She sits there and keeps asking "Is it over yet?" and whines all night.

KEVIN: Trouble in paradise?

DANNY: You'll understand when you've been with Michelle as long as I have been with Susan. It gets old.

KEVIN: Never. Not with a girl like Michelle.

DANNY: Ah, the innocence of first love. Makes me want to puke.

KEVIN: Listen, I am sorry I forgot, but I am going with Michelle tonight.

DANNY: Fine, whatever.

KEVIN: Call Susan, take her.

DANNY: Yeah, I guess. What a drag.

KEVIN: Get used to it. Michelle and I are going to be spending a lot of time together.

DANNY: Maybe we can double sometime, huh?

KEVIN: That's an idea.

DANNY: How about tonight?

KEVIN: What about your game tickets?

DANNY: See, that's the beauty of this idea. Michelle and Susan can go shopping while we go to the game, and then we'll meet them afterward.

KEVIN: Out. Get out.

DANNY: Hey, call me tomorrow and tell me how it went with Michelle.

KEVIN: OK.

DANNY: I want ALL the details.

KEVIN: OUT!

AFTER THE INTERVIEW

BERT: Seventeen years old, a varsity football player.

BRYCE: Also seventeen, also on the varsity team.

RYAN: Same as Bert and Bryce, but in charge of the committee for Homecoming Queen.

SETTING: Scene opens with Ryan sitting alone on stage, depressed, holding in his hand a small slip of paper. Bryce and Bert enter and go to him.

BERT: Hey, big Ry. What you got there?

RYAN: The list of girls who made it for Homecoming Court . . . and the Queen.

BRYCE: You've got that? Let me see it. *(He reaches for it.)*

RYAN: I can't let you see it. It's supposed to be a secret. And besides, you don't want to know this queen.

BERT: Ryan, it can't be that bad.

RYAN: Want to bet?

BRYCE: Come on. Who are we going to tell anyway.

RYAN: Just the entire school is all. I know you guys. You two will start taking bets on who the winner is and . . .

BERT: Come on, big guy. We wouldn't do that. Scout's honor.

RYAN: You were never a scout.

BRYCE: Just tell us.

RYAN: I shouldn't trust you two.

BERT: Don't be a wuss, Ryan.

RYAN: Shut up, Bert. *(He looks at them, they try to look honest and angelic. RYAN shakes his head in disgust.)* **Well . . .**

BRYCE: Just whisper it.

RYAN: Funny Bryce. OK. Well, you know it came down to the final three, right?

BRYCE: Right.

BERT: Yeah, it was Cilla, Teri, and Diane.

BRYCE: Only the three meanest girls on campus.

RYAN: *(Handing the slip of paper to BRYCE)* **Remember, it's not my fault.**

BRYCE: Oh no. Bert, look.

BERT: *(Seeing the name, almost falling to the ground.)* **Ohhh. I don't believe it.**

BRYCE: Ryan, how did you let this happen?

RYAN: I told you, it's not my fault. I did everything I could to make the other judges hate her.

BERT: She's probably the most hated girl on this campus.

BRYCE: No doubt. Of the three, she's the worst.

RYAN: I know. I can't stand her. I don't know why those guys voted for her.

BRYCE: Probably because she is dating Tim.

BERT: What's Tim got to do with it?

BRYCE: She's his girlfriend and he's the team captain. Not to mention the biggest guy at school. Would you want him mad at you?

RYAN: You should have seen her resume. Loaded. She's done so much community service, it's not funny.

BERT: Yeah, I've heard about her community service.

BRYCE: You said it, man.

RYAN: I can't stand this girl.

BRYCE: Ryan, who else knows about this?

RYAN: What do you mean?

BRYCE: Who else knows the name of the winner?

RYAN: Just me. I counted the votes.

BERT: Wasn't Mr. Garcia supposed to be there?

RYAN: He had a phone call . . . He told me to count them and to tell him the name when I was done. I'm going over to his office right now.

BRYCE: *(Smiling evilly)* **So we three are the only ones who know the name of the winner.**

RYAN: Yeah, I guess so.

BRYCE: *(Looking at BERT)* **Are you thinking what I'm thinking?**

BERT: Oh, yes.

RYAN: What? . . . *(Realizing what the plan is)* **No way, man. No way would I do that. I could get in so much trouble.**

BRYCE: All we have to do is change one little name on that slip of paper.

BERT: Yeah! We could have the Queen be anyone we want. We could make it be Suzanne.

BRYCE: She didn't even go out for Queen.

BERT: We could say it was a write-in vote. Queen by popular demand!

RYAN: That's stupid. Who would believe that we could have a write-in Homecoming Queen? Besides, I know I'd get caught.

BERT: Who's going to know?

RYAN: Mr. Garcia.

BRYCE: But you said that you haven't told him the name yet, so what's the problem?

RYAN: I'll get caught.

BRYCE: So what? What's the worst that could happen?

RYAN: I could get suspended.

BERT: A small price to pay for the honor of your school.

RYAN: Shut up. Forget it, guys. *(Holding up the paper)* **She is our queen. We have no choice.**

BERT: You're a wuss Ryan. I can't believe you have an opportunity to fix this and you won't take it.

RYAN: Hey, it's not my fault.

BRYCE: It is if you can do something about it and you don't.

RYAN: *(Looking at the name)* **She's not that bad.**

BERT and BRYCE: She's a bitch.

RYAN: I know. All three of them are.

BRYCE: And she's the biggest.

BERT: Her mom doesn't have Alpo delivered to the door for nothing, you know.

RYAN: Well, she was the one chosen, and there is nothing I can do about it.

BRYCE: You mean, nothing you WILL do about it.

RYAN: Whatever.

BRYCE: Well, there's one good thing about this whole business, Bert.

BERT: Yeah? What's that?

BRYCE: That we will be in the locker room when he has to crown her.

BERT: I hear you.

RYAN: Guys . . .

BRYCE: Let's go, Bert.

BERT: See ya, Ry. Have a good time crowning this queen.

RYAN: Thanks a lot, guys. *(BERT and BRYCE exit laughing. RYAN looks at the name and exits in depression.)*

SHELLY

MIKE: 17

CHUCK: Also 17, Mike's best friend.

SETTING: Mike enters the room, Chuck, on the phone, motions to Mike to take a seat on the bed.

CHUCK: I don't know ... Maybe... Well, what do you want? ... Shelly, do we have to go into this now?... OK... Because Mike is here and... No, that's not what we're going to do... Hey, why don't you just hire a private detective to keep an eye on me...No...Fine...I swear, Shelly, I don't know what it is you want from me...Listen, we'll talk later...Mike is here I said and he...Hello? Hello? *(Hangs up.)* **Jeez.**

MIKE: Problems?

CHUCK: Very funny.

MIKE: Just trying to lighten the mood. Really, is she hassling you again?

CHUCK: Mike, just back off, OK? I don't need it tonight.

MIKE: Whatever. *(They sit for a few seconds in silence.)* **Well, I can see we're in for an exciting evening's entertainment.**

CHUCK: You know, I just don't know what the girl wants from me. I try to be nice, then I get treated like dirt. I get tired of that so I give dirt back and then she says I'm cheating on her.

MIKE: I don't know why you take this crap. She isn't worth it.

CHUCK: I love her, OK?

MIKE: Why? She's mean to you, she hates me and I'm your best friend.

CHUCK: She thinks that you try to get me to go out on her.

MIKE: Yeah, that's it. I have nothing better to do with my life than to break you and Shelly up.

CHUCK: She's jealous of the time we spend together.

MIKE: Come on, man. That's just stupid. You need time with your friends. If she had a brain under all that make-up, maybe she'd understand that.

CHUCK: I told you to back off.

MIKE: Just stating a fact, man.

CHUCK: Listen, I don't want you saying anything against her.

MIKE: I'm not. It's just that ever since you started going with her, she is the main thing in your life. Football school, work, everything takes a back seat to what that . . .

CHUCK: Hey . . .

MIKE: Sorry, to what SHE wants. Including our friendship.

CHUCK: What does that mean?

MIKE: Nothing. Forget I said anything. Are we going or are we staying?

CHUCK: We're going after we stay and talk about this.

MIKE: About what?

CHUCK: What you just said. Our friendship. Shelly coming between us.

MIKE: Why bother? This is old territory and we've been through it before.

CHUCK: What does that mean?

MIKE: What it means is that last year when you first started going with Shelly you completely ignored the fact that you have a friend, you spent every minute with her, we never went out like buddies are supposed to do.

CHUCK: We went out all the time.

MIKE: No. We doubled with me going out with Shelly's friends who were not girls I would choose.

CHUCK: I thought we had some great times.

MIKE: No, you had some great times with Shelly, exploring the many facets of young love. I and my date sat in the other room listening to the sounds you two made.

CHUCK: Great. Very nice.

MIKE: Chuck, face it, we almost stopped being friends. Shelly hated my guts because she couldn't stand for you to be with anybody but her.

CHUCK: Maybe it's because every time we did go out together, we did some heavy partying, some dancing, and some major scamming on girls. She had reason to be mad.

MIKE: Chuck, we're 17 years old. That's what we were supposed to do.

CHUCK: Well, you can understand then why Shelly still doesn't like you, right.

MIKE: And you can understand why I hate the b--

CHUCK: I told you not to call her that.

MIKE: Call her what you want, she is what she is. I swear, you were so much better to hang out with when you guys finally broke up. You were . . . I don't know . . . a guy again.

CHUCK: What was I before we broke up.

MIKE: Whipped.

CHUCK: Thanks a lot.

MIKE: I don't know why you are even thinking of getting back together with her. Look at you. You're tense, you're arguing with her over the phone and you haven't even gone on a date yet.

CHUCK: I don't know what to do. She calls all the time, she cries, tells me she loves me. The hard part is I still love her, too.

MIKE: Do you?

CHUCK: What does that mean?

MIKE: Did you ever think that maybe what you miss isn't Shelly, but is something that she gave you?

CHUCK: Man, it isn't the sex. Sex I can get from anybody.

MIKE: Heck, I don't know then. Because I sure don't see it. All I see is my best friend starting all over with a girl who did nothing but make him miserable.

CHUCK: Man, I don't know.

MIKE: Me either. *(The phone rings, they both look at it.)* **Chuck, you do what you have to do. See her or don't, but no matter what, I'm your friend.**

CHUCK: *(Picking up jacket)* **Let's go.** *(They start to exit, MIKE leaves first, CHUCK looks back at ringing phone, walks out.)*

THE JERK

CHRIS: Sixteen years old, has finally reached the point of no return with his best friend's manner of life style.

STEVE: A sixteen year old insensitive clod, caught up in his own needs, completely disregarding the feelings of his family and friends.

SETTING: The scene takes place in Chris's bedroom. It is empty when Steve enters, all full of angry emotions.

STEVE: *(Enters in an angry rush, calls out.)* **Chris, are you in here?** *(Throws himself in a chair.)* **I can't stand it anymore.**

CHRIS: *(Enters, sarcastically.)* **Hey, make yourself at home.**

STEVE: Are you ready for this? They took away my car. Can you believe it? My car!

CHRIS: Your parents took away your car?

STEVE: No, the tooth fairy took away my car. Yes, my parents.

CHRIS: Why?

STEVE: They say it's because of my grades.

CHRIS: What do you mean "They say?"

STEVE: It's not my grades. It's just another one of their power trips. Another way to show me that I'm the kid and they are the adults.

CHRIS: What were your grades, anyway?

STEVE: Chris, my grades are not the point. You are missing the point entirely.

CHRIS: So, what is the point.

STEVE: I told you. It's power. My parents are into this major power struggle with me. That can't stand to see that I'm becoming a man, that I'm not their little boy anymore.

CHRIS: Oh . . . So, what were your grades, just out of

curiosity.

STEVE: Two "C's" three "D's" and "F" and one "A".

CHRIS: The "A" was in P.E., right?

STEVE: Yeah, so?

CHRIS: Nothing.

STEVE: So, what? You think I'm wrong.

CHRIS: I didn't say anything, Steve. I'm just sitting here, listening as usual.

STEVE: What does that mean?

CHRIS: It means that I'm listening. That's what you want me to do, right? Listen?

STEVE: You're acting like it's some big chore or something.

CHRIS: No, I'm just listening. You want someone to talk at, so here I am.

STEVE: And what does that mean? Talk "at"?

CHRIS: You know, you always do this. You get mad at someone or something, you come over here and spill your guts and then you leave. I'm supposed to just sit here and let you vent your anger? OK, so vent.

STEVE: I don't get it. I came over here to talk to someone I thought was my best friend. Why, all of a sudden, are you acting like this?

CHRIS: Don't ask questions you don't want honest answers to.

STEVE: What? Are you saying that you can't be honest with me?

CHRIS: Yeah, I guess that is what I am saying.

STEVE: Well, maybe you better come right out and say what you are thinking.

CHRIS: Yeah, I think I will. Steve, we have been friends for a long time, right?

STEVE: Since seventh grade, almost five years now. I thought that . . .

CHRIS: Hey, I'm the one who is supposed to be talking,

remember.

STEVE: *(Irritated)* **Fine, talk.**

CHRIS: **For the last few years I have seen you change from the really nice guy I used to know into this . . . I don't know.**

STEVE: *(Proudly)* **Rebel?**

CHRIS: **Rebel. What does that mean to you?**

STEVE: **Someone who won't put up with crap from people just because they are older and think they are smarter. Someone who can think for himself.**

CHRIS: **Yeah, rebel. A rebel without a clue is more like it.**

STEVE: **Hey . . . !**

CHRIS: **You have been acting like a jerk, Steve, a real jerk. You cut classes all the time, you get lousy grades, you are rude to everybody, you drink too much. You're a jerk. And I'm getting sick of it.**

STEVE: **Thanks a lot. You're a great friend. Fine, you feel that way, I can hang with someone else.**

CHRIS: **Who?**

STEVE: **Mark, Brian, Rick, lots of people.**

CHRIS: **Yeah? Were you out with them last night?**

STEVE: **They all had to work.**

CHRIS: **You think so?**

STEVE: **Are you telling me they didn't?** *(CHRIS nods.)* **You're a liar. You don't know anything.**

CHRIS: **I know they didn't work last night, because we all went to Julie's party.**

STEVE: **Julie had a party? I didn't hear about it.**

CHRIS: **It was private. Only people she wanted to be there were invited.**

STEVE: **So, I wasn't invited. Why?**

CHRIS: **Because you're a jerk. You didn't used to be, but you sure are now. I'm your best friend, I don't even like you much.**

STEVE: *(The reality of the situation hitting him.)* **Julie had a party, huh?**

CHRIS: It was fun, too.

STEVE: Didn't anybody ask where I was?

CHRIS: We all knew you weren't going to be there. Most people have gotten really tired of your attitude, your mouth and just plain you. It was pretty much a group decision.

STEVE: So why hasn't anybody said anything before this?

CHRIS: They did, you just never listen to anybody but yourself. That's another thing everybody is tired of, you talking about yourself all the time.

STEVE: So, what do I do now?

CHRIS: I don't know. Everybody is pretty tired of you . . . including your parents.

STEVE: My parents?

CHRIS: Yeah, they called me last week and were telling me how they can't seem to get through to you and could I help. I guess that's what finally made me decide to talk to you like I am. I mean, if your own parents are starting to dislike you, you're in big trouble.

STEVE: I guess so. So, what do I do?

CHRIS: I don't know. Stop being a jerk, I guess.

STEVE: How? I don't even know what I'm doing that is jerky.

CHRIS: Maybe that's the problem. You are so caught up in thinking how cool you are, you don't give much thought to what anybody else is feeling.

STEVE: So, what do I do?

CHRIS: Stop it.

STEVE: How?

CHRIS: I don't know.

STEVE: *(Gathering his jacket up.)* **Let's go.**

CHRIS: What?

STEVE: I'll buy you dinner and you can tell me how I am being a jerk. You've got nothing else to do, right?

CHRIS: See, that's what I mean. You automatically assume that I have nothing else to do. Well, I do. Rick and I are going to a club in about an hour.

STEVE: Well, I'll go with you guys. *(CHRIS turns his head away.)* **Rick doesn't want me to go.**

CHRIS: Yeah.

STEVE: *(A low whistle.)* **Wow. Well, are you busy tomorrow?**

CHRIS: Not as far as I know. I'll call you.

STEVE: Yeah, call me. Maybe I'll go home and talk to my parents.

CHRIS: Maybe you should. You need a ride?

STEVE: No, I've got my car.

CHRIS: I thought you said your parents took it away.

STEVE: I drove it anyway. They are at work.

CHRIS: What a jerk.

STEVE: *(Finishing the sentence with him)* **. . . jerk. Yeah I know. See you later.**

CHRIS: OK. *(STEVE leaves.)* **What an ass.** *(Shakes his head.)*

MOVING OUT

MICK: Eighteen years old, still living at home and chafing under the restrictions put on him by his parents.

JON: Also eighteen, but working, going to college and living on his own.

SETTING: Mick is on the phone when the scene opens. Jon is busily cutting carrots, celery, etc., for party guests. The scene goes on with the two continuing food preparations.

MICK: *(Hanging up the phone, furious.)* **Fine. Just fine.** *(He slams down the phone.)*

JON: What now?

MICK: My mother. She wants me home at 11:00.

JON: Eleven? Tonight? Are you sure she didn't mean 11:00 tomorrow morning?

MICK: Very funny. C'mon.

JON: What do you mean, "C'mon"?

MICK: Well, I've got to leave, so let's go.

JON: Mick, I don't have to be home by 11:00. You do. I am staying. The party is just beginning and I don't feel like leaving now. Hand me that celery.

MICK: What are you doing?

JON: I told James I would help him with the food for this party, and I am helping. You said you'd help, too.

MICK: That was before my mom said I had to get home.

JON: Whatever. You want to get those crackers so I can put this disgusting whiz stuff on them. I can't believe people eat this stuff.

MICK: You're staying?

JON: I told you I was.

MICK: Then how do you plan on getting home? You came in my car.

JON: Maybe I'll just stay at Steve's house tonight. Why did you even call your mom, anyway?

MICK: Because she wants to know where I am when I leave from one place to another.

JON: Oh, brother.

MICK: She worries.

JON: That is just stupid. You're not a child anymore.

MICK: Try telling her that.

JON: I don't see why you put up with it.

MICK: What choice do I have?

JON: Just tell her. Say, "Mom, I am 18, in college now, not high school."

MICK: Then she'll come back with the old, "My house, my rules" line.

JON: I don't know why you put up with it.

MICK: Believe me, I have thought many times of just running away. Maybe if I shake her up, she'll realize the problems.

JON: Running away?

MICK: Yes. Just one day take a bag of clothes, hop into my car, and take off for about two weeks. No note, nothing. Just leave.

JON: Mick, that's just stupid.

MICK: Why? It would do my mom good to have a little bit of a scare. Maybe she'd realize how wrong she is to treat me this way if she thought I had taken off.

JON: Mick, running away is stupid.

MICK: How would you know what it's like? You've always had a great relationship with your parents.

JON: That's because they trust me. I wouldn't do anything stupid like run away. Besides, my parents and I talk. We communicate.

MICK: Fine, then I will talk to her and see what happens. But if that doesn't work, I'm out of there.

JON: Fine, but you don't run away.

MICK: What do you mean?

JON: Mick, you are 18, You're in college. You move out.

MICK: Move out?

JON: Yes. You say, "Mom, Dad, I am moving out." Children run away. Adults move out.

MICK: But, Jon, then it would be for real.

JON: Well, what do you want?

MICK: I want to stay out past 11:00 without having to get permission or feel guilty for not calling.

JON: Then move out.

MICK: But how?

JON: You just do it. I did it.

MICK: But you work.

JON: That's also part of being an adult.

MICK: Wow. Move out, huh?

JON: You know, Sean is planning on getting married to Rita next summer, so they're thinking of moving in together now. You can take his room if he does move in with her, that way I don't have to look for a new roommate.

MICK: Sean is getting married?

JON: Yeah. To Rita.

MICK: But he's only a few years older than us.

JON: He's 21. When he gets married, he'll be 22.

MICK: *(Quietly)* Married. Wow.

JON: It's what grownups do. That and move out.

MICK: But how could I? I mean, I go to college.

JON: So do I. I work and go to school.

MICK: But that's almost all you do.

JON: I have fun . . . not as much as you, but I have responsibilities.

MICK: How many hours do you work during a week?

JON: Usually 30, sometimes 40.

MICK: Jeez, that's almost full time, plus school.

JON: Yeah, but I like it. I live on my own, don't answer to anyone. And I don't have to be home at 11:00.

MICK: My mom would freak if I told her I was moving out.

JON: Think again.

MICK: What does that mean?

JON: I was talking to your mom last week, when I called and you were at the mall . . . spending HER money, I might add. We had an interesting little talk.

MICK: What did she say?

JON: She asked me when I thought you would finally grow up and get out. Believe me, she wants you out as bad as you want to leave. Probably more so.

MICK: I can't believe that. Why would she say that?

JON: Because you need to grow up. The only reason she has you call and she wants you home early is because she worries. If you moved out, she wouldn't have to worry because you would be gone.

MICK: She WANTS me to move out?

JON: All parents feel that way after a while.

MICK: If I decided to, you're sure I could move in with you?

JON: As long as you follow the rules.

MICK: Very funny.

JON: I'm not kidding.

MICK: What rules?

JON: Don't leave your garbage all over the place, leave my clothes alone, provide your own food, clean up the kitchen, no dishes left in the sink, turn off lights when you leave a room . . .

MICK: I might as well stay at home.

JON: Yeah, and there it's free. Your part of the rent would be $255 a month, not including utilities.

MICK: I'd have to work.

JON: It's called growing up. It happens to all of us.

MICK: So, Sean is really going to get married?

JON: So he says.

MICK: Twenty-two? Married? It seems like yesterday we were all still in high school.

JON: It was only last year, Mick.

MICK: Yeah, but things are getting so different.

JON: Things change. People change. Have you seen Kara lately?

MICK: No. Is she coming tonight?

JON: I think so.

MICK: I'm calling my mom and telling her I'm staying a little longer. I want to see her. And you and I can talk about me moving in.

JON: Sounds good.

MICK: *(Going to the phone)* **Kara, I haven't seen her since she graduated. That was, what, three years ago?**

JON: She's changed.

MICK: How? Greatest body on the cheer squad in the history of the school. And beautiful.

JON: She's still beautiful. Has that certain glow about her.

MICK: What glow?

JON: The one pregnant married ladies get at about the sixth month.

MICK: What?

JON: Like I said, we change.

MICK: *(Laughing)* **I guess so.** *(Into the phone)* **Hi, mom?**

LEAVING

CHAD: Fifteen years old, troubled and confused by the turmoil he feels inside.

DEVIN: Chad's eighteen-year-old brother, trying to understand the trouble inside of Chad, but frustrated by not being able to help.

CHAD: *(Off-stage)* **Just leave me alone. God, just get out of my way and leave me alone.**

DEVIN: *(Off-stage)* **Don't walk away from me, Chad, I am talking to you. Chad, get back in here.**

CHAD: *(Entering the room, throwing things into a bag.)* **That's it, brother. I am out of here. I am getting as far away as I can and going as fast as I can.**

DEVIN: *(Following him in)* **What? What is the problem?** *(Seeing him pack things)* **What are you doing?**

CHAD: Isn't it obvious? Don't you see me packing my things? Are you a moron? I am leaving.

DEVIN: OK. I see clothes flying, I hear you yelling. But you have done nothing to explain it. You just scream and yell and say "I'm leaving, I'm leaving."

CHAD: You know, that's part of the problem around here. No one ever listens to anything I say. And Devin, you are as guilty as the rest of them!

DEVIN: Wait. I listen. It's just that I'm not hearing anything that makes any sense. And the rest of who? What are you whining about?

CHAD: I don't need you to join in on this official Dump on Chad week, you know.

DEVIN: Wait, what do you mean, "Dump on Chad week?" Who's been dumping on you? *(Grabbing him and sitting him down.)* **Sit down and talk to me.**

CHAD: Why? Because you'll listen? Right. *(Pulling away)* **I am sick of you, of this family, of everything. I've**

just got to get away.

DEVIN: Away to where? Where? Just what do you think you're going to do? And where are you going to do it?

CHAD: I don't know. I don't care. Just outta here.

DEVIN: Fine. Do what you always do. Run away from a problem. God forbid you should ever sit down and discuss anything. Oh no. Chad, poor misunderstood, mistreated Chad. You know something? I know that you're upset. I don't know what about, but I know that you're upset. The problem is that lately, that's all you are anymore is upset.

CHAD: What the heck does that mean?

DEVIN: What it means is that for the last several months you have been nothing but a grey cloud over this house. You never smile, you sit in a ball on the couch clutching the remote control like a life preserver, sipping a coke, talking to nobody.

CHAD: Why talk when all I get is negative response, like now? I am very upset, my life is hell and you don't listen, you just preach.

DEVIN: What are you upset about? I swear, I don't know. You have a great life, a great family, a great home. What is your problem?

CHAD: I don't know. I just know that I'm depressed all the time. I feel completely unloved.

DEVIN: I am so sick of you saying that. Nobody loves me. Nobody understands me. What do you want from us?

CHAD: *(Yelling)* **I want some understanding for once.**

DEVIN: *(Yelling back)* **What do you want me to understand?**

CHAD: *(Yelling)* **I don't know.** *(Quieter)* **I don't know.**

DEVIN: *(After a silence)* **What is wrong, Chad?**

CHAD: *(After a silence)* **I really don't know.**

DEVIN: I don't get it.

CHAD: That's why I am upset. I don't know what I'm upset about. I cry all the time and I don't know why. Everything makes me feel like crap. I feel like I am falling apart and no one is there to help me.

DEVIN: Chad, we are all here, all you have to do is ask for help.

CHAD: But every time I try to talk to you or mom and dad, all I get is a lecture on how lucky I am and what a great family I have and how I should be grateful. I know all that, but for some reason, I don't feel better. I feel . . .

DEVIN: What, what do you feel?

CHAD: I don't know. I feel trapped. And unhappy. And angry. Really angry. And I don't know why.

DEVIN: Is it me?

CHAD: Partly.

DEVIN: What? What did I do to make you angry?

CHAD: Devin, that's just it. I don't know. It's just sometimes I look at you and think, "Get out. Get out of my room. Get out of my life."

DEVIN: *(Quietly)* **Thanks.**

CHAD: No, you don't understand. You aren't listening.

DEVIN: You said you want me out of your life.

CHAD: That's just it. That's what I'm saying, and that's what you're hearing, but you aren't listening to hear what I really mean.

DEVIN: What are you talking about? Get out is a pretty clear statement.

CHAD: That's not what I mean, though. I think I mean me. I want me to get out.

DEVIN: You mean move out? Is that what you mean?

CHAD: No. I mean actually get out.

DEVIN: What?

CHAD: I think I'm starting to think about getting out of life.

DEVIN: That's not funny. That's not amusing. That's just stupid.

CHAD: *(Beginning to leave)* **Why do I bother?**

DEVIN: Hey, don't get mad at me. I just think what you said is pretty darn selfish and stupid.

CHAD: I'm trying to explain to you how I ***feel*** **and I don't need judgments.**

DEVIN: I'm sorry, but I just find that kind of thing stupid.

CHAD: Forget it. Forget I said anything.

DEVIN: I don't want to forget it. I want to know what's wrong.

CHAD: I told you. I don't know. You obviously don't understand it anymore than I do, so forget it. Just forget it.

DEVIN: Chad, I can't. What, you mean you're going to kill yourself?

CHAD: No, I just mean . . . I don't know, I . . . I just don't know.

DEVIN: Chad, you need help. You need more than I or mom and dad can give you.

CHAD: I just need to be left alone.

DEVIN: That's the worst thing for you. You need to talk to somebody that knows about these things.

CHAD: *(Exhausted)* **Just leave me alone, Devin, just leave me alone.**

DEVIN: I can't. You need help. More than I can give.

CHAD: *(Curling into a chair)* **I need to be left alone.**

DEVIN: *(Watching him for several seconds and then quietly leaving.)* **Damn.** *(Taking another look and again quietly.)* **Damn.**

CHEATING

TOM: A fun-loving and irresponsible seventeen year old, just getting by in life and school.

SAM: Much more responsible in his attitude towards school and life, has become irritated with Tom and his "using" people.

SETTING: Takes place wherever the director decides it takes place. Sam is sitting by himself, and Tom enters in a frenzy.

TOM: Sam, I have been looking all over for you.

SAM: Why?

TOM: Wait till I tell you about last night.

SAM: Ooohooo? You went out with Diana, right?

TOM: Get a clue, my young friend. I finished with Diana last week. No, I was out with Lara.

SAM: Who is Lara? And why are you finished with Diana?

TOM: Lara is small, gorgeous and lives on her own in L.A. while Diana is none of those things.

SAM: So, you dump Diana and now you have L.A. Lara. Where did you meet her?

TOM: At the Hard Rock Cafe, last night.

SAM: Last night? Last night was a Tuesday. Your mom let you go to L.A. on a Tuesday night?

TOM: No, she let me go over to your house.

SAM: But, you said you . . . oh.

TOM: Did you get your Econ finished?

SAM: Yes, why?

TOM: I didn't have time to do it, so let me look at yours, OK?

SAM: Wait a minute. You want my homework?

TOM: I'm not speaking a foreign language, here. Yes, I want your homework.

SAM: Let me get this straight. You dump Diana, you don't even tell me . . .

TOM: Sorry, I didn't realize I had to clear my social life with you before I could change women . . .

SAM: That's not the point.

TOM: Then what is the point?

SAM: OK, skip Diana.

TOM: I already did.

SAM: You tell your mom that you are going over to my house and you go to L.A.

TOM: I'd do the same for you.

SAM: The point is, I wouldn't ask you to.

TOM: Fine, don't take advantage of the opportunity I offer to you.

SAM: And now you want my Economics homework.

TOM: You always let me copy your assignments.

SAM: You've noticed that, have you?

TOM: Lighten up, Sammy-boy, and just let me see your stuff.

SAM: Wait a minute. ME lighten up?

TOM: What is your problem?

SAM: Who'd you go to the Hard Rock with?

TOM: Just Brian and Krista.

SAM: So, the three of you trooped down to L.A. and didn't even call me?

TOM: Could you have come?

SAM: You know I can't go out late on school nights.

TOM: Then why should we have called you?

SAM: It would be nice to at least think I was included. Besides, it would be nice to know that if you were going to use me in a lie, I should at least be aware of it.

TOM: I didn't even think about it.

SAM: What a shock.

TOM: Besides, why get you upset? And you don't even like Brian that much anyway.

SAM: You don't either. Why do you hang out with him, anyway?

TOM: He's got a car. I needed a ride, he was there. Geez, what is the problem?

SAM: Why don't you just ask Brian for HIS Econ work?

TOM: Because he usually copies from me.

SAM: Wait a minute . . . You mean that when you finish copying my work, you hand it over to Brian and he copies it?

TOM: He copies mine, not yours.

SAM: But you copy mine.

TOM: But when he copies it, it's my paper.

SAM: With my work.

TOM: What is the big deal?

SAM: For all I know, the entire class is handing in my work. I could be getting the grades for everyone at school.

TOM: Don't be an idiot. Just let me see it. *(They look at each other for a moment.)*

TOM: So, are you going to let me see your work?

SAM: No.

TOM: What? I told you I need to use it.

SAM: I think use is the right word.

TOM: And what is that supposed to mean?

SAM: Well, you used Diana until you found someone better, you use Brian 'cause he has a car, and you use me because I got good grades in Econ.

TOM: Come on, you're getting ridiculous. I don't use anybody.

SAM: Think about it, Tom.

TOM: I'll tell you what I'll think about. I'll think about getting better friends.

SAM: Friends? Tom, would you even be over here if I didn't get good grades?

TOM: Yes.

SAM: I don't think so. I also don't think I even like you, you know that? Or myself.

TOM: What does that mean?

SAM: I think I'm only friends with you because you're "popular." We're not friends at all. We're both users.

TOM: Fine, we're both rotten users. Let me use your work.

SAM: Today I will. *(He hands it over to TOM, who begins copying quickly.)* **But no more. I don't want to do this anymore. It doesn't feel right.**

TOM: So you're saying it would "feel right" if we were better friends? Isn't that a little hypocritical?

SAM: I don't know. I guess. But I do know that I am not doing your work for you anymore.

TOM: *(Furiously copying)* **Whatever. Does this mean you don't want me telling my parents that I'm over at your house when I'm not?**

SAM: You could say that, yes.

TOM: And you don't want to go out with me on the weekends?

SAM: I didn't say that.

TOM: I thought you said we weren't friends.

SAM: Not like real friends. More like party partners.

TOM: Party partners. I can live with that. Think we could ever be real friends?

SAM: *(As they are walking off.)* **Probably not.**

REHEARSAL

RYAN: The director of the scene, annoyed with his two scene mates because they won't work.

BOBBY: One of the actors in the scene for drama one. Wants to work, but is irritated with the whole situation.

EDDY: "Hey, it's just drama one, who cares" is the byword of this boy.

SETTING: The stage is bare for a moment when Ryan enters carrying two chairs. He calls off stage to Bobby and Eddy.

RYAN: *(Entering the stage)* **Let's go in here. There's no one in here and we can get some work done.**

BOBBY: Fine with me.

EDDY: Me, too.

RYAN: Let's start at the top of the scene and run it through from there.

EDDY: Why don't we start from where we left off yesterday?

RYAN: Because I am the director and I want to start at the top.

BOBBY: I can feel a power trip coming on.

RYAN: No power trip here. We just have work to get done and for once I'd like to get a decent grade on a scene.

EDDY: Whatever, man.

RYAN: You know, Eddy, what I don't understand is why you are even in this class.

BOBBY: Ryan, just kick back, OK?

RYAN: Bobby, you kick back before I kick your butt, OK?

EDDY: What is with you? Lately all you do is jump all over us. It's just a stupid drama scene, for god's sake.

RYAN: Like I said, Eddy, why did you take this class? You bring down every scene you are in.

EDDY: It's drama, guy, not calculus. We don't need it to graduate.

RYAN: Then why didn't you take something else? Like ROP?

BOBBY: Can we just get going here?

EDDY: Really. Let's just start this stupid thing.

RYAN: Fine. Get where you're supposed to be at the top of the scene.

EDDY: *(Moving to his spot)* **I'm here, right?**

RYAN: You don't know?

BOBBY: Jeez.

RYAN: Bobby, do you know where you're supposed to be?

BOBBY: At lunch.

RYAN: Funny, Bob, very funny.

BOBBY: You asked.

EDDY: You know, we ARE giving up our lunch for you.

RYAN: It's your grade, too. And if you two had worked in class we wouldn't be here at lunch trying to save this scene.

EDDY: What do you mean, "If you two had worked?" Are you saying you did?

RYAN: At least I had my stuff ready to go. all of my blocking was done on the first day. You still don't have your lines memorized and we go on next period.

BOBBY: My lines are memorized.

RYAN: Since when?

BOBBY: Last night. My mom worked with me.

RYAN: Well, at least I can count on you.

EDDY: Hey, I'll be fine up there. My natural talents will bring it all together.

RYAN: Bull. What are you planning to do? Improvise your lines?

EDDY: I've got the general gist of what they are.

BOBBY: Just be sure to give me my cue lines, OK?

EDDY: Bobby, my man, you should not feel so hung up on the written word. It should merely be a springboard for your natural talents to shine.

RYAN: Oh shut up and let's try this from the top, OK?

EDDY: I'm ready.

BOBBY: Do you think that this once we could run it without you stopping us every other line, Ryan?

RYAN: I'm the director, I'm supposed to direct you.

EDDY: You know, you are always blaming us for this scene not coming together. I think it's your fault, not ours.

RYAN: What?

EDDY: Seriously, look how many times have we been through it without stopping? Bobby, tell him.

BOBBY: Never.

EDDY: See?

RYAN: That's because you never do it how I want it done.

EDDY: Did it ever occur to you that how you want it done isn't the right way?

RYAN: But I am the director.

BOBBY: I don't think that makes you god, does it, Eddy?

EDDY: Not the last time I checked the bible.

RYAN: This is stupid. Just get where I told you to be at the start of this and let's go.

EDDY: Just trying to give some helpful hints, my friend.

BOBBY: *(Getting into character of Felix in Odd Couple)* **"Oscar, where have you been? I called the office, no one answered."**

EDDY: *(As Oscar, but forgetting his line.)* **"I, uh . . . are you finished? Then smile . . ."**

RYAN: Oh fine, that's just great. So you cut the whole scene and skip to the end . . . two lines into it.

BOBBY: Come on, Eddy, you know the lines, don't you?

EDDY: I'm telling you, I'll be fine in front of an audience.

RYAN: You are going to suck in front of an audience.

EDDY: Listen, man . . .

BOBBY: No, you listen.

EDDY: *(Surprised at this sudden outburst from quiet BOBBY.)* **Excuse me?**

BOBBY: You listen, you jerk.

RYAN: Tell him, Bobby . . .

BOBBY: You shut up, too. I'm sick of both of you and your arguing. This may "just be drama" to you, Eddy, but I like it and I took it because I like it. I also care about my grades.

RYAN: Me, too, Eddy . . .

BOBBY: And you, big mouth, you do nothing but complain. I swear if you had spent half of the time you put into arguing and whining into actually directing this scene, maybe we'd have something.

RYAN: Hey, just a minute . . .

BOBBY: No, you wait just a minute. I am sick of listening to you two bitch at each other, like a couple of freshman girls. You either get it together right now, or I walk. And if I walk, this scene will definitely get an "F".

EDDY: Bobby, it's just drama one.

BOBBY: Obviously you just don't care. *(Turning to RYAN)* **I say we kick him out of the scene, ask the teacher for an extra day and work on this tonight at my house.**

RYAN: You want to?

BOBBY: I don't want to fail this class.

RYAN: OK with me. What time?

BOBBY: Right after school?

RYAN: Can I get a ride with you?

BOBBY: Meet me at my car after sixth period.

EDDY: Wait a minute.

RYAN: What?

EDDY: **What about me?**

RYAN: *(Looking at BOBBY who nods approval)* **You're fired. Come on, Bob, lets go talk to the teacher.** *(They leave the stage, EDDY stands alone.)*

▪ MIXED ▪

BIG BROTHER

JOSH: Eighteen years old, getting ready to leave for college, but at the moment quite disappointed in his younger sister.

CARRIE: Fourteen years old, about to enter high school, she is a young woman waiting to happen.

SETTING: Carrie enters the room as Josh is packing his suitcase.

CARRIE: Has mom come in yet?

JOSH: Not yet.

CARRIE: Oh. I just wondered.

JOSH: I bet you did.

CARRIE: So, you haven't talked to her, huh?

JOSH: Not yet.

CARRIE: Are you going to?

JOSH: Talk to her? I would imagine so. After all, I am leaving for college and she is driving me to the airport. I would think that sometime between now and getting on the plane we will talk.

CARRIE: Yeah, I guess you will.

JOSH: Yes, I guess we will.

CARRIE: Are you almost packed?

JOSH: Do you really care?

CARRIE: Should I?

JOSH: I don't know . . . should you?

CARRIE: I guess not.

JOSH: Then don't hang around in my room getting in my way.

CARRIE: Fine. *(She leaves)*

JOSH: *(To the empty space)* **Fine.** *(He continues to pack.)*

CARRIE: *(Entering the room again)* **This is yours.** *(She hands him a sweater.)*

JOSH: *(Taking it)* **Thank you.**

CARRIE: I'm finished with it.

JOSH: That's fine.

CARRIE: It's a warm sweater.

JOSH: It always kept me warm.

CARRIE: You'll need it back east.

JOSH: Yes, it gets cold. *(He still has not looked at her.)*

CARRIE: Maybe I should put it on now.

JOSH: Why?

CARRIE: It's awfully cold in here.

JOSH: Who's fault is that?

CARRIE: Josh, I said I was sorry. I can't say much more than that.

JOSH: Well, that's too bad, because "I'm sorry" doesn't begin to cover it.

CARRIE: So, you're going to leave mad?

JOSH: Carrie, I'm not mad. I'm disappointed . . .

CARRIE: Oh, please . . .

JOSH: Not to mention a little scared.

CARRIE: Scared? What of?

JOSH: Of you, or should I say of what I can see you becoming?

CARRIE: What is that supposed to mean?

JOSH: Your actions at my going-away party last night. Your drinking for one thing.

CARRIE: Excuse me, big brother, but you downed more than a few beers yourself.

JOSH: Yes, but I am 18, you are 14. Therein lies the great chasm between us.

CARRIE: Josh, please don't go "college" on me. I hate when you talk that way. You sound like an ass.

JOSH: Then, I just won't talk to you, how's that?

CARRIE: OK, I'm sorry. I shouldn't have had anything to drink. But there's more to it, isn't there?

JOSH: You're darn right there is.

CARRIE: What?

JOSH: Glenn.

CARRIE: **So what? I went for a drive with him. Big deal.**

JOSH: **He had been drinking.**

CARRIE: **He wasn't drunk. He wasn't even buzzed. He told me he just had a couple of beers . . .**

JOSH: *(Finishing the sentence with her)* **. . . couple of beers. Right. To Glenn, a case is a couple of beers. But that's not even the main point. The main point is Glenn himself.**

CARRIE: **I thought he was your best friend.**

JOSH: **I thought so too. But, now I don't know.**

CARRIE: **But why?**

JOSH: **Because he took my little sister out at 2:00 a.m. when she had been drinking too much. And I know his reputation. I've been on double dates with him and I know what he does with girls. He's a slime.**

CARRIE: **You always said he was cool.**

JOSH: **That was before he took my 14-year-old sister out.**

CARRIE: **We didn't go out. We went for a drive. As a matter of fact, he was telling me how much he is going to miss you . . . his best friend.**

JOSH: **And where were his hands during this conversation?**

CARRIE: **On the steering wheel. C'mon, Josh. Glenn thinks of me like his own little sister.**

JOSH: **That's why every time he comes over here he says "Incest is best."**

CARRIE: **He's just being funny.**

JOSH: **I don't like it.**

CARRIE: **So, is that why you got into a fight with him in front of everybody and called him those names? And yelled at me?**

JOSH: **Yes. That's why.**

CARRIE: **And it had nothing to do with the fact that you'd been drinking quite a bit yourself?**

JOSH: **I only had a couple of beers . . .**

CARRIE: . . .couple of beers. Uh huh.

JOSH: OK, so maybe I had too much to drink. But that isn't the point here.

CARRIE: What is?

JOSH: The point is, I'm leaving today. And you'll be starting high school in a few weeks.

CARRIE: Yes. So?

JOSH: So, I'll be gone and Glenn will still be here.

CARRIE: For heaven's sake, Josh, he's a senior. I'm just some lowly freshman.

JOSH: And freshman girls are considered fresh meat by the senior guys. I know. I was a senior guy this last year, remember?

CARRIE: Are you saying you got together with a freshman girl? Who? Is it anybody I know?

JOSH: Let's just leave it at the fact that I know what the guys do . . . and how they talk. I don't want you to be the topic of any locker room conversation.

CARRIE: Who . . . come on, tell.

JOSH: Carrie, I'm very serious. Once a girl gets that kind of reputation, she's trashed her entire high school life. That isn't what you want, is it?

CARRIE: No.

JOSH: Then listen to me and trust what I am saying. Don't get into a car with Glenn.

CARRIE: Ever?

JOSH: Ever.

CARRIE: How about if he wants to give me a ride home?

JOSH: Only if it is still light out . . . even then, it makes me nervous.

CARRIE: Is he really that bad?

JOSH: Remember Michelle?

CARRIE: That tramp? Yes.

JOSH: Why do you call her a tramp?

CARRIE: Well, Glenn told me . . . oh.

JOSH: You see? You're not even in high school yet and you already know the gossip.

CARRIE: Oh dear.

JOSH: I told you.

CARRIE: How come, though, people talk bad about Michelle, but no one says anything but how cool Glenn is?

JOSH: I'll share this secret with you, but only because you're my baby sister and I am worried about you.

CARRIE: Yes?

JOSH: Men are pigs. Never forget that.

CARRIE: Even you?

JOSH: To some girl's big brother, yes, I am a pig. It's not a nice thing to admit, but puberty does strange things to a senior.

CARRIE: Men are pigs.

JOSH: Just keep saying that till I get home at Christmas. I'll escort you to the parties, but until I'm here to keep an eye on you, your freshman year should be spent on your studies.

CARRIE: Yeah, right.

JOSH: Well, at least promise to be home before midnight on the weekends.

CARRIE: That I can do.

JOSH: And stay out of Glenn's car.

CARRIE: How about Mikey's?

JOSH: When did he get his license?

CARRIE: Yesterday. He turned 16 last week.

JOSH: Still a dangerous age. But he's young enough to be somewhat fearful of my anger. OK, you can see him.

CARRIE: Thanks.

JOSH: And not a word of any of this to Mom. I don't think she could handle it well at all.

CARRIE: You've got my word on that one. *(She holds out her hand to shake.)*

JOSH: *(He hugs her.)* **I'm gonna miss you, little girl.**

CARRIE: Me, too.

JOSH: Carry this bag out to the car, I'll take the suitcase.

CARRIE: Hey, Josh . . .

JOSH: Yeah?

CARRIE: Thanks for caring.

JOSH: It's a dirty job, but somebody's got to do it.

BREAKING UP IS HARD TO DO

SANDY: A nice girl . . . which may be her problem.

JIM: The actor must remember that Jim is not arrogant, just confused about his feelings.

SANDY: *(From kitchen)* **Jim, you want anything?**

JIM: *(In living room)* **Just you.** *(Shakes his head to himself.)*

SANDY: Funny. Really, can I get you anything?

JIM: No, I'm fine.

SANDY: *(Entering)* **Yes, you certainly are.**

JIM: *(Patting couch for her to sit.)* **C'mon and sit with me.**

SANDY: *(Does)* **I love you.**

JIM: I know.

SANDY: *(After a moment of silence)* **I know? That's an odd response to "I love you."**

JIM: I know.

SANDY: The correct response is: "I love you, too."

JIM: I know . . . *(Sighs)*

SANDY: Why do I get the feeling I'm in for a lousy way to end this evening.

JIM: I don't know . . . . *(Quietly)* **I do love you.**

SANDY: Why does that not sound very reassuring?

JIM: What do you mean?

SANDY: I love you. The way you said it. It sounded more like "I'm fond of you."

JIM: Sandy, we've been together for almost a year. I think I've proven myself to be more than fond of you.

SANDY: Yes . . . but . . .

JIM: What?

SANDY: Nothing.

JIM: I hate when you do that.

SANDY: I'm sorry.

JIM: I also hate it when you say you're sorry all the time.

SANDY: I'm sorry.

JIM: Sandy, stand up for yourself.

SANDY: I try, but everytime I do you get mad.

JIM: I do not. It's just that you can be such a doormat sometimes. It bugs me.

SANDY: It seems like everything I do lately bugs you.

JIM: *(Silence for a moment)* **What were you going to say?**

SANDY: When?

JIM: Before.

SANDY: Before what?

JIM: *(Irritated)* **Before you went into your usual doormat routine.**

SANDY: Geez. What is with you tonight?

JIM: I don't know what you're talking about.

SANDY: It seems like you are just begging for a fight.

JIM: Oh, that's it. Blame me.

SANDY: I'm not blaming anyone.

JIM: Everytime it ends up like this lately.

SANDY: Everytime what ends up like what and since when?

JIM: You. You pick at everything I say.

SANDY: You know, I get the feeling we are having a fight, but you just forgot to let me in on it.

JIM: Don't play dumb with me.

SANDY: WHAT ARE YOU TALKING ABOUT?

JIM: All I said was I love you and you jump on it like a dog after a bone.

SANDY: *(Shaking head, at a loss)* **I do not know what you are talking about.**

JIM: You accused me of not loving you.

SANDY: I didn't. *(Confused)* **Did I?**

JIM: Fine, now deny it.

SANDY: I'm not denying anything.

JIM: So you admit it.

SANDY: ADMIT WHAT?

JIM: That you think I don't love you?

SANDY: No... I mean yes... I mean... What are we talking about here?

JIM: Whether or not I love you.

SANDY: You do . . . don't you?

JIM: *(Silence)*

SANDY: Don't you?

JIM: *(Pause)* **Yes, I love you.**

SANDY: *(After a second)* **I think I remember what we were supposed to be fighting about.**

JIM: What?

SANDY: The "I love you."

JIM: *(Quietly)* **What about it?**

SANDY: It sounds like you *(Put hand in downward motion)* **love me. Not like you** *(Hand in upward motion)* **love me.**

JIM: *(Not looking at her)* **I don't know what you mean.**

SANDY: That's why you've been so hard to be with lately. You don't love me anymore.

JIM: I do love you.

SANDY: But are you "in love" with me? *(Silence from JIM)* **I thought so.**

JIM: *(A long pause)* **I didn't know how to say it.**

SANDY: So you tried to make me miserable by fighting with me all the time?

JIM: No. I just . . . I don't know. I don't want to hurt you.

SANDY: Honesty would be nice.

JIM: I am being honest. I do love you. I'm just not . . .

SANDY: *(Puts finger on his lips.)* **Don't say it. Just don't say it out loud.**

JIM: Not saying it won't make it untrue.

SANDY: *(Quietly)* **Please leave.**

JIM: I can't. I don't want to leave it like this.

SANDY: Like what? What do you want me to do? Smile, shake hands, wish you well? Fine. I wish you well, now just leave, please.

JIM: Sandy, I love you. I don't want you to be hurt. I

don't want to see you cry.

SANDY: Then leave, cause I'm about to.

JIM: I'm sorry. Really.

SANDY: I know. Me too.

JIM: I do love you. We will always be friends.

SANDY: No, we won't.

JIM: But why?

SANDY: I can't handle that. I can't go from lover to friend in that short a time period. You have obviously had time to get used to the idea. I don't think I ever will.

JIM: But . . .

SANDY: Go. Please. I can't have you here right now.

JIM: I don't understand why you want me to leave.

SANDY: Because I'm going to cry, and I don't want to do that in front of you.

JIM: I've seen you cry before.

SANDY: But not over you. And you never will. Goodbye, Jim.

JIM: I'll call you tomorrow.

SANDY: Goodbye.

JIM: *(A pause)* **Goodbye, Sandy.** *(He leaves.)*

SANDY: *(Runs hands over face, through hair, then quietly.)* **Jerk.**

CHOICES

SHARON: Eighteen, soon to graduate from high school. Full of wonderful expectations for the future.

TONY: Sharon's boyfriend, also eighteen, filled with dreams and hopes, but facing frustration about achieving them.

SHARON: Two more months. I don't know if I can take any more than that.

TONY: *(Preoccupied)* **Tell me about it.**

SHARON: Graduation, summer, and then we are gone. Tony, are you as excited as I am?

TONY: Thrilled.

SHARON: Yeah, I can tell. Tony, what's the matter?

TONY: Nothing. Everything is fine.

SHARON: No, I can tell something is the matter. What is it?

TONY: There is "nothing the matter." God, what a stupid phrase.

SHARON: Listen, I know something is wrong. You are trying to start a fight with me. Well, we've been through this little plot line too many times, and I am not following it. When you feel like opening up, let me know. *(She continues what she was doing.)*

TONY: *(After a moment's brooding)* **Sharon, I'm leaving.**

SHARON: Fine. Call me when you're in a better mood.

TONY: No, I mean I am leaving-leaving.

SHARON: Me? You're leaving me? Because I don't want to fight with you this time and stand up for myself, you want to break up?

TONY: No, no, that's not what I mean.

SHARON: *(Grabbing him, holding him close)* **Don't scare me like that, please, ever again. I don't know what I would do if I lost you.**

TONY: I was hoping you'd say that.

SHARON: Was there ever a doubt I wouldn't?

TONY: But I am leaving. After graduation, I'm getting out of this town.

SHARON: Well, we both are. We're going to go away to college together. I know you're frustrated now, especially because the end is so near, but gut it out. It will be here before you know it.

TONY: Sharon, sit down. Stop flitting all over the room and listen to me.

SHARON: *(Finally looking at him, seeing he is very serious.)* **What? What are you leaving? What are you talking about?**

TONY: This. I am leaving this life. *(SHARON gasps, putting her hand over her mouth.)* **No, no. I mean** *(He waves his hands around.)* **this. This kind of life.**

SHARON: What kind of life?

TONY: The kind of life our parents live. The nine-to-five what's-for-dinner-honey kind of life. I can't do it.

SHARON: I still don't know what you mean. You won't have that kind of life with me. We'll go to college, we'll be professionals, *(Attempting a small joke)* **we'll have a maid to ask what's for dinner.**

TONY: It's the same thing. *(Grabbing her by the arms, sitting her down.)* **Don't you see? We'll end up like our parents. We get married, buy a house, have 1.4 children, tell them to turn down the music. That's the worst thing that could happen. Telling them to turn down the music.**

SHARON: So, we'll put them in a soundproof room.

TONY: I don't mean that music. I mean the music of life.

SHARON: You're talking in riddles. Say what you mean.

TONY: For once, Sharon, look beyond today. Really look and see what the future is holding out to us. Look for the path not taken, and it will make all the difference.

SHARON: Please don't quote dead poets to me. Just talk. Say exactly what is going on with you . . . with us.

TONY: I'm leaving, but I'm not going to college . . .

SHARON: What . . .?

TONY: Let me finish. I'm going to New York.

SHARON: Why New York? What's there?

TONY: Music. All kinds of music and music producers. I've got so much music inside of me that it hurts from trying to burst free.

SHARON: This is crazy. I don't get it. Why do you have to let your music "burst" in New York? Can't you study music in college? Major in it.

TONY: It's not something you study. Music is something you either have or you don't. I have it. I've got to do something with it. In New York I can be free of my parents, of everyone I've known all my life, of . . .

SHARON: Me. You can be free from me.

TONY: No. That's another thing. Come with me. With you standing behind me, supporting me, there's nothing I can't do.

SHARON: But what about college? What about my future?

TONY: Your future is with me. College is a dream that belongs to our parents. Do you really want to go? I know I don't.

SHARON: I don't know. I guess I could go to college in New York.

TONY: After a while, when I make it, of course you could. We'd work together to make it happen.

SHARON: What do you mean, "After a while"?

TONY: One of us would have to work while I was making the rounds of producers and studios.

SHARON: One of us is me? I would have to work? What about you?

TONY: I need to work on my music. It would be a twenty-four-hour-a-day effort.

SHARON: What about your parents? Won't they help out?

TONY: I don't want to have to depend on anybody.

SHARON: But me.

TONY: I'd be doing this for both of us. For our future. For our dream.

SHARON: Your dream. Tony, this is your dream.

TONY: It could be our dream if you'd let it.

SHARON: My dream includes college. My dream is to be a lawyer.

TONY: You could have your dream . . . just a little later. By that time I'll need a good business lawyer to handle my affairs. Don't you see how this could work for us?

SHARON: I want to be a defense lawyer, not a business lawyer.

TONY: You're missing the whole point of this discussion. Go with me, Sharon. Come to New York. I need you with me. Walk the path not taken.

SHARON: I don't want to lose you. But . . .

TONY: Marry me.

SHARON: What?

TONY: Marry me. Come to New York and marry me.

SHARON: Ohh. I've dreamed of this moment. Yes! I'll marry you. I'll follow you to New York. *(She jumps in his arms.)*

TONY: *(Holding her)* It will be great. You and me, taking on New York. I can do anything with you there to lean on, to support me.

SHARON: And I will be there for you.

TONY: Mr. and Mrs. Anthony March. *(Looking at her, holding her face.)* How does that sound? Mrs. Anthony March.

SHARON: *(Pauses, looking at him, really seeing him.)* **Mrs. Anthony March.** *(She moves away from him, pauses, faces him again.)* **Mrs. Anthony March?** *(Quiet deep breath)* **Wow.**

TONY: You and me.

SHARON: And your dream.

TONY: Our dream.

SHARON: No, Tony, your dream. I just fit into it. Mrs. Anthony March. Breadwinner. Supporter of husband. Worker bee.

TONY: You're seeing this wrong.

SHARON: No, I'm seeing reality. You're the one with the dream. It's a good dream, Tony, but it's yours. I just got swept up in the riptide effect.

TONY: Don't you love me?

SHARON: More than you know. But I love me, too. I love being the person I am. I'm not Mrs. Anthony March. My name isn't Anthony . . . that's yours.

TONY: You're being grammatical.

SHARON: I'm being who I am . . . a realist. I can't be Mrs. Anybody until I try to be all I can be.

TONY: Then join the army.

SHARON: Weak joke.

TONY: I'm sorry. *(Looking at her)* **Sorry about a lot.**

SHARON: Don't be. It's a nice dream. You should go to New York but not with me. Give your dream a try, and I will work for mine.

TONY: It won't be the same without you.

SHARON: You're right. You'll have to work.

TONY: That's not what I meant.

SHARON: I know. I know. It's not what I meant, either. I mean that you'll have to work harder on your dream because it will be ***your*** **dream.**

TONY: So, does this mean we break up?

SHARON: I don't know. I think it just means we take

our own paths, alone. But we'll always be there for each other.

TONY: Just miles apart.

SHARON: You can look at it that way. I prefer to think of it as a phone call away.

TONY: *(Holding her)* **I will always love you.**

SHARON: No matter where we end up? *(He nods.)* **Me too.**

DOES IT MATTER?

ROBERT: Seventeen years old, upset about the death of his friend and confused about his friends' lack of feelings.

MATT: Also seventeen, more accepting of the "life goes on" school of thought.

AMY: Seventeen, appears to be very self-absorbed, but is a realist about life and expects it from others.

SETTING: A funeral reception for a friend who has committed suicide.

ROBERT: Did you look?

MATT: At what?

ROBERT: At . . . her.

MATT: You mean . . . oh. Nah.

ROBERT: I did. Whew.

MATT: How'd she look?

ROBERT: Dead, I guess. She looked dead.

MATT: Makes sense. She was.

ROBERT: She looked good, though.

AMY: *(Entering on ROBERT's last two words.)* **Who, me?**

MATT: No, Jackie did.

AMY: You mean I don't look good?

MATT: Who cares how you look? Today isn't about you.

AMY: I care. You know I like to make a good presentation.

ROBERT: A little self-absorbed today, Amy, even for you.

AMY: I prefer to think of it as self-aware. Have you tried the onion dip?

MATT: No. Is it good?

ROBERT: Both of you are just too much. Jackie is dead and *(Indicating AMY)* **you're talking fashion and** *(Indicating MATT)* **you're feeding your face.**

MATT: I'm hungry. Funerals make me hungry.

ROBERT: Everything makes you hungry.

AMY: Listen, we paid our respects, let's get out of here.

MATT: I'm with Amy. This place is dead. Oooops.

AMY: *(Laughing)* **No kidding. Let's go.**

ROBERT: For God's sake, Jackie is dead. At least pretend you have some respect for that fact.

AMY: Listen — I told you I never liked the girl. I think if I leave it would show a lot more respect than if I stayed. In fact, I think it's a little hypocritical for any of us to be here.

ROBERT: She's dead, Amy.

AMY: *(Gathering her things)* **Yes. Well. I suppose that's too bad. But it was her own carelessness that killed her, don't you agree, Matt?**

MATT: What? Oh, yeah, I guess so.

ROBERT: I thought she was your friend.

AMY: We partied together. We weren't best friends. I never called her in the dark of night to share any intimate secrets, if that's what you mean.

MATT: So, what do we do about this summer? Are we still on for the beach house?

ROBERT: We probably won't go.

AMY: Because Jackie's dead? Oh, brother. We can get another person to take her place for her part of the rent.

ROBERT: You mean you'd still go?

AMY: In a hot New York minute. And so will everybody else.

ROBERT: I don't think so.

MATT: *(Quietly)* **I'm still going.**

ROBERT: *(A gasp of surprise)*

AMY: You want to ride with me?

MATT: When are you leaving?

AMY: Let's see. Thursday I'm getting my nails done at 10:00 and then I have to stop at Nordstrom's to pick

up a dress I'm having altered. I can get you after that.

MATT: Could we stop and pick up my board at my cousin's house?

AMY: You want to bring that tatty old surfboard? *(He nods.)* I suppose so.

ROBERT: I cannot believe you two. You're making vacation plans at Jackie's funeral reception. Do you see something kind of shallow and mean-spirited in that?

AMY: In what? In that life goes on and so do we? Come on, Robert. You know you feel like we do.

ROBERT: No, I don't.

AMY: Well, you will.

ROBERT: Maybe this is why she killed herself. Because no one in this world cares about anyone but themselves.

AMY: Get real, Robert. You say I'm selfish. What she did is about as selfish and self-centered as you can get.

MATT: Her mom said in her note Jackie said that she felt there was too much trouble in the world for there to be any point in living.

AMY: Selfish.

ROBERT: Maybe her death will make a difference.

AMY: Only that there's one less person in the world to stand behind in any lines.

ROBERT: You are a cold-hearted bitch.

AMY: No, I'm realistic. Look, she's been dead three days. I'll admit, the first day I was as upset and shocked as anyone else. I mean, dead at 17.

MATT: Me, too. I was really upset. Only the old are supposed to die.

AMY: Exactly, but then, a couple days go by. At first, it was all anyone talked about. Now, here we are at her funeral and we're making summer plans.

ROBERT: But don't you feel bad that you didn't take

the time to really know her?

AMY: No. But I do feel bad that she took the time away from me before I could get to know her. So, what's been accomplished by her dying?

ROBERT: I don't know. I've been thinking and thinking about why she would do this.

AMY: I'll tell you what's been accomplished. Nothing. Oh, we'll all talk about it for a while; some, like you, even longer than just a while.

MATT: But, like she says, life goes on.

AMY: You know what the saddest part is? Think about ten years from now, say at our high school reunion. I would bet that someone says "Remember that girl that killed herself?" She'll be "that girl." And the only people that really care, her family, are left with nothing but wondering what they did wrong.

ROBERT: So, in other words, she lived for nothing, and she died for nothing.

MATT: It sure seems as if she died for nothing, because nothing will change, everyone still goes on.

AMY: But did she live for nothing? We'll never know, will we? She never gave herself a chance.

ROBERT: I wish I could have said something to her.

AMY: I wonder if it would have made a difference.

MATT: Like you said, who knows?

AMY: You ready to go?

MATT: Anytime you are.

AMY: Then let's go.

ROBERT: Hey, wait up.

AMY: You coming with us?

ROBERT: Yeah. I'm going with you.

AMY: *(Putting her arm around him)* **I knew you would. C'mon.**

GRADUATION

EDDY: A high school senior, happily anticipating college acceptances. Feels he has a clear idea of where he is headed.

MARCIE: Also a high school senior, has decided on a different path than Eddy and is now making it known to him.

SETTING: This scene can take place wherever the director chooses. Be sure that the actors have a specific task to complete while they are acting this scene.

EDDY: It's here, it's here.

MARCIE: What?

EDDY: My college acceptance. Yes!!

MARCIE: Where'd you apply?

EDDY: Everywhere, but I want Stanford, and I got it.

MARCIE: Wow, Stanford. I am impressed.

EDDY: As well you should be. *(Grabbing her and dancing her around the room.)*

MARCIE: Eddy, what are you doing?

EDDY: Dancing out my happiness. *(He leans her back in a deep dip.)*

MARCIE: Listen, Fred Astaire, put me down. *(He does)* **So I can assume from this ridiculous display of joy that you are pleased with this?**

EDDY: *(Kissing the letter)* **My acceptance to Stanford.** *(Dancing happily around the room, sing-song the following)* **I am going to Stanford. I am going to Stanford. I won't be stuck going to a junior college.**

MARCIE: Eddy, please, that's enough.

EDDY: Did yours come yet?

MARCIE: Uh, no . . .

EDDY: *(Suddenly embarrassed)* **Oh, Marcie, I wouldn't worry. I mean with your GPA, you'll get in.**

MARCIE: I wouldn't count on it.

EDDY: Don't be so down. I know you said you were applying to UCLA and Berkeley, but I hear they sometimes send out their acceptances late.

MARCIE: Eddy, I'm not going to get any acceptances from there.

EDDY: You don't know that.

MARCIE: I didn't apply.

EDDY: You what?

MARCIE: I didn't apply.

EDDY: You're going to the JC? I can't believe you'd settle for that.

MARCIE: No, I'm not going to the JC.

EDDY: What, then . . .? Mechanics school?

MARCIE: Don't be stupid, Eddy, or they might take away your ticket to Stanford.

EDDY: You don't be stupid. What happened?

MARCIE: I didn't apply.

EDDY: You what?

MARCIE: I didn't apply.

EDDY: Why not?

MARCIE: Because I decided I don't want to go to college. At least not right now.

EDDY: What are you going to do? Be a bum?

MARCIE: I'm going to give acting a shot.

EDDY: Get real, Marcie.

MARCIE: I am. I really mean this.

EDDY: That's the stupidest thing I have ever heard in my life.

MARICE: Thanks.

EDDY: Hey, it is. You're throwing away your future for ACTING?

MARCIE: I'm good. You know I'm good.

EDDY: Yeah, you're good. So is every other high school senior who had the lead in the plays at school. That's only about 5000 girls.

MARCIE: But not all of them are going to try.

EDDY: No, they are going to DO something with their lives. They are going to college.

MARCIE: At least I'm doing something I believe in. I'm not just going to college because I can't figure what else to do with my life like some people I could mention.

EDDY: Me, you mean?

MARCIE: You said it, not me.

EDDY: I have a reason to go to college.

MARCIE: Yeah, what?

EDDY: Because I want a future . . .

MARCIE: So do I . . .

EDDY: I mean a realistic one.

MARCIE: So, what are you going to major in?

EDDY: Social Ecology.

MARCIE: Social what?

EDDY: Ecology.

MARCIE: So, after four years, what do you do then?

EDDY: I get my master's.

MARCIE: Two more years . . . then what?

EDDY: My PhD.

MARCIE: So in 8 to 10 years you have a PhD in Social Ecology. Now what do you do?

EDDY: I become a psychologist or a lawyer or something.

MARCIE: Or something. That's just great.

EDDY: At least I have a goal.

MARCIE: So do I.

EDDY: Oh yeah, acting. *(In a snooty voice)* **You're going to be an AHCTOOOR. What are your chances?**

MARCIE: The same as anyone else's. Maybe better.

EDDY: Why can't you try and go to college at the same time?

MARCIE: Because I don't want to. I want to concentrate

on the one thing I know I am good at.

EDDY: You can major in Drama.

MARCIE: Oh fine, and then be stuck taking all those stupid general education classes I don't give a rat's behind about. I don't care about Physics or Trig. I don't need those to be an actor. Heck, I don't need those for anything when you think about it.

EDDY: I can't believe I am having this conversation. Have you told your parents about this?

MARCIE: Yes, I have.

EDDY: And they have agreed to this stupid idea?

MARCIE: Let's not say they are thrilled, but they understand and will support me.

EDDY: They are going to support you?

MARCIE: Emotionally. Not monetarily. They said they would support college, but not this. They said that if I felt strongly enough to do this, then I would have to work for it.

EDDY: That makes sense.

MARCIE: It doesn't to me. They would support me going to college and wasting my time taking classes I care nothing about, but they won't give me money to try what I do want.

EDDY: It's their money.

MARCIE: Yes, they have made that abundantly clear. They did tell me they are going to keep a college fund there for me for when I "come to my senses," as they put it.

EDDY: What are you going to do?

MARCIE: I've got some interviews in Hollywood with some agents set up already. I took some pictures, too. Want to see?

EDDY: I guess so. *(He looks at them.)* **Not bad.**

MARCIE: I also got a job.

EDDY: A what? A job? Marcie Seton with a job?

MARCIE: I've got to pay for acting classes.

EDDY: What are you doing?

MARCIE: Demonstrations. I stand in those booths at conventions and promote their products. "Hi, I'm Marcie. Would you like to try our new laser shoe polisher." You know, that kind of stuff.

EDDY: You're really serious about this, aren't you?

MARCIE: Yes, I am.

EDDY: I don't feel quite so grown up anymore.

MARCIE: Me, either. It's scary.

EDDY: I think I'm going to miss high school. *(Looks at MARCIE.)* **Nah.**

OVER WITH

JAY: Sixteen and pretty sure that he's a terrific guy, loved by one and all . . . or so he thinks.

PAM: Also sixteen, spent a brief period in a relationship with Jay for which she still has some anger.

SETTING: In the quad area of a high school. It is early morning, warm, before the first class of summer school.

JAY: Let's get it over with.

PAM: Fine, I don't want to be here anymore than you do.

JAY: God, I hate summer school.

PAM: Well, you should have thought of this before you signed up.

JAY: Signed up, right. My mom signed me up.

PAM: Why didn't you just tell her "No"?

JAY: You've met my mother.

PAM: Good point.

JAY: It's so darn hot out here.

PAM: You are always hot.

JAY: You should know. *(He wiggles his eyebrows in comic suggestiveness.)*

PAM: No wonder you're here for summer school. You must want to catch up on your ancient history.

JAY: Oh, you miss me and you know it.

PAM: Yes, about as much as I miss listening to you sing every time you feel the need.

JAY: You love the way I sing.

PAM: I'd like it better if you could hit the occasional note and perhaps stay on pitch once in a while.

JAY: Very nice.

PAM: Let's just go, OK? I really don't feel like walking down this path again.

JAY: What path?

PAM: The path that starts off with you getting me into a

"vibing" match with you for fun, and then ends with one of us being hurt or angry.

JAY: What are you talking about?

PAM: Listen Jay, we just started being friends again after that stupid "relationship" we had, and I don't want to go into all of that crap we went through.

JAY: God, you are so sensitive lately. PMS?

PAM: Jay, don't start.

JAY: Start what?

PAM: Jay, I'm serious. I will walk right out to the parking lot, get in my car and leave your sorry self here to face summer school alone, if you say one more word.

JAY: Fine. Fine. Not another word.

PAM: Good.

JAY: Fine.

PAM: Good. Now let's go in.

JAY: *(Raising his hand.)*

PAM: You may speak . . .

JAY: I . . .

PAM: But watch it.

JAY: I'm sorry.

PAM: Good. Let's go.

JAY: No, really, I'm sorry. Pam, I mean it.

PAM: *(She looks at him questioningly.)* **Do you?**

JAY: I do. I didn't mean to turn our friendship into a joke. I want you to know that.

PAM: It wasn't a joke, exactly. Jokes are funny. Us as a twosome was definitely not a laugh-a-minute.

JAY: Pam, c'mon, we had some fun.

PAM: Oh, yeah. It was really fun putting each other down in front of all of our friends. It was fun waiting for you to finally show up all of the times you were late picking me up. My favorite fun part was watching you watch other girls.

JAY: I was the way I always was. You just started getting all tense about it. Why?

PAM: Why, Jay? Why? Because you don't "vibe" a girlfriend, Jay. You don't come half an hour late without calling a girlfriend, Jay. You don't watch other girls walk by with your girlfriend standing right next to you, Jay. That's why, Jay. OK?

JAY: I'd like to thank you for clearing that up for me, Pam.

PAM: Fine.

JAY: Good.

PAM: Fine.

JAY: So, hey, I'm glad we're back to being friends. Aren't you?

PAM: *(Sarcastically)* **Oh, hey, it's swell.** *(They sit in silence for a bit, sneaking glances at one another. JAY smiles and then PAM slowly does the same.)*

JAY: Face it, we're better friends than lovers.

PAM: You can say that again, especially with you.

JAY: Oh, unkind. *(They laugh for a moment.)* **I wasn't bad, was I?**

PAM: What do you mean?

JAY: You know? The lover part?

PAM: We didn't do enough for me to make that kind of judgment.

JAY: Well, hey, for the sake of research . . . *(He reaches for her.)*

PAM: No, thanks. We'll let the question go unanswered.

JAY: But now you'll never know.

PAM: I'll live. *(They smile at each other, almost starting to hug, but don't.)*

JAY: C'mon, summer school and computer class await.

PAM: My life is a full one.

JAY: Of course, I'm in it.

PAM: The ego of the man. Let's go if we're going.

SIBLINGS

BOBBY: A big brother concerned about his "little sister's" ability to deal with men.

LINDA: His 15-year-old sister "just growing up," but confident.

CAST: The entire scene takes place in Linda's bathroom. Most of it will probably be played to each other in the mirror. Linda should be putting on finishing touches while Bobby messes with her stuff.

BOBBY: *(Calling from Off-stage)* **Linda, where are you?**

LINDA: *(Calling out)* **I'm in here.**

BOBBY: *(Entering)* **Hi. Whatcha doin'?**

LINDA: Getting ready.

BOBBY: *(Looking at her)* **You better hurry. You haven't got that much time.**

LINDA: I'm almost done.

BOBBY: You are? Oh.

LINDA: What? Bobby, what? *(Looking at herself in the mirror)*

BOBBY: Nothing. Is that what you're wearing?

LINDA: You don't think I should?

BOBBY: I didn't say that. I just asked you if that is what you plan to wear.

LINDA: Well, I've got it on, so I guess I had planned to wear it.

BOBBY: Oh.

LINDA: Oh again? What is it with the "Oh"?

BOBBY: Nothing.

LINDA: It's not dressy enough, is it?

BOBBY: No . . . I didn't say that.

LINDA: You don't have to. I can see it in your eyes. I look like the pig of the forest, don't I?

BOBBY: Linda, you look fine, honest.

LINDA: Really?

BOBBY: Yes. How are you going to do your hair?

LINDA: It's done.

BOBBY: Oh.

LINDA: Oh? Oh again?

BOBBY: Calm down, Linda. You look great.

LINDA: Why are you here? Did you come in here just to drive me crazy?

BOBBY: I came in here to help you get ready.

LINDA: Robert, thank you, but your kind of help I don't need. You are making me crazy.

BOBBY: So, I'll just sit here and talk.

LINDA: About what?

BOBBY: About tonight.

LINDA: Rules review?

BOBBY: Just a brief one.

LINDA: *(Looking skyward)* **Oh Lord, give me the strength to get through this night without killing him.** *(Back at BOBBY)* **OK, rule number one, both feet on the ground at all times.**

BOBBY: And why?

LINDA: Because if both feet are on the ground, nothing can happen . . . unless you are very limber.

BOBBY: That's not funny, and I am sure Mom wouldn't think so either.

LINDA: Out! Get out of my bathroom and let me get ready.

BOBBY: When we're done with the review of the rules . . . until then, put on your eye stuff.

LINDA: You mean mascara.

BOBBY: What ever you call that black crud.

LINDA: It's on!

BOBBY: Oh.

LINDA: OH! What is it with you and oh? Darn it, what did I do with that mascara?

BOBBY: Rule number two?

LINDA: *(Paying no attention to him, touching up her eyes.)* **Carry money.**

BOBBY: Why?

LINDA: *(Getting exasperated)* **In case Rick wants to get wild, I can chip in for the room at the Big Six Motel and Grill.**

BOBBY: Linda, are you going to take this seriously or not?

LINDA: NOT. Bobby, this is stupid. I am fifteen years old, not five. I can take care of myself.

BOBBY: OK, you're fifteen, but it's your first real date . . . in a car with a guy who's almost 18 . . .

LINDA: He turned 17 last week, and I will be 16 next month.

BOBBY: That is beside the point.

LINDA: Would you please tell me what the point is so I can get ready without you standing here the whole time.

BOBBY: The point, my innocent, naive, young sister is, I know what guys are like. I too, am a guy.

LINDA: So? Rick is a lot like you.

BOBBY: Then you are definitely not going out with him.

LINDA: The difference is, I am not like the bimbos you prefer to associate with . . .

BOBBY: Bimbos? Who have I ever gone out with that was even a little bimbo-like?

LINDA: Does the name Erin ring a bell?

BOBBY: Erin is a nice girl. Warm, friendly . . .

LINDA: Yeah, friendly with about half of the football team.

BOBBY: Which brings me to my other point . . . Rick is part of THAT half of the team. *(His eyebrows wiggle meaningfully.)*

LINDA: What? He . . . with Erin? *(BOBBY nods.)* **Oh, you**

don't know for sure. And they say women gossip.

BOBBY: It ain't gossip when it's true.

LINDA: Were you there? Did you SEE anything?

BOBBY: I heard that . . .

LINDA: You heard. Forget it then. Heard . . . you should hear what they say about you.

BOBBY: Like what?

LINDA: You are a male tramp.

BOBBY: For a guy, that's not so bad. But you are a girl, and my little sister. I don't want anyone talking like that about you.

LINDA: Bobby, I am touched by your concern, but please, get out of here so I can finish.

BOBBY: Where is he taking you?

LINDA: First to dinner and then we might go to the beach.

BOBBY: The beach?

LINDA: Is something wrong with that?

BOBBY: Only that the beach is the biggest make-out place in the world.

LINDA: *(A sly smile)* **Is it?**

BOBBY: What does that mean?

LINDA: I know what the beach is, Bobby, and I intend to have a very goooood time.

BOBBY: You are not leaving this house.

LINDA: Don't be ridiculous. There, how do I look?

BOBBY: Fine, but a little overdressed to stay at home, 'cause you are not going out with some jerk who plans on taking my little sister to the beach to do god knows what.

LINDA: Get a life, Bob. *(The doorbell)* **He's here.**

BOBBY: Old Richard and I are going to have a little chat before you two leave.

LINDA: Don't you dare.

BOBBY: I'm not going to embarrass you. I just want to

talk to him for a minute. *(He pushes up his shirt sleeves and exits.)* **Hey, Rickster, you're taking out my little sister, huh? Let's talk.**

LINDA: *(Alone On-stage)* **I'm dying. First I'm going to kill him and then I am going to die.** *(As she exits.)* **Hi, Rick. Ignore my brother. He's been off his medication for too long.**

SUSPENDED

SAMMY: 15 years old, upset and angry.

JESSE: 14 years old.

JESSE: *(Sees SAMMY enter room, throws books on floor, collapses on chair.)* **Problem?**

SAMMY: Shut up, Jesse.

JESSE: Sheesh, what a grouch.

SAMMY: Shut up, Jesse.

JESSE: Fine. *(A moment's silence while JESSE watches SAMMY moodily stare into space.)* **Sammy, what's wrong?**

SAMMY: Nothing. *(Goes to book bag, takes out paper, looks, crumples it and throws it across room.)* **Absolutely nothing.**

JESSE: *(Looking at paper on floor)* **I can see that.**

SAMMY: Shut up, Jesse.

JESSE: Hey, I didn't do anything to you, so you can change your attitude towards me, OK? Be mad, but don't take it out on me.

SAMMY: Why don't you just shut your mouth.

JESSE: Why don't you say that a little louder, so mom can hear. She's right in the next room.

SAMMY: *(On way out, stops.)* **Mom is home?**

JESSE: Yes.

SAMMY: God, I can't get a break.

JESSE: Sammy, what is your problem? You act like you are headed for prison or something.

SAMMY: I may as well be.

JESSE: What is going on?

SAMMY: If I tell you, you promise not to go running to mom and dad like you usually do whenever I tell you something?

JESSE: I promise.

SAMMY: *(Looking closely at JESSE)* **Forget it.**

JESSE: No, really, I promise. But what if I do? They are going to find out anyway.

SAMMY: Yeah, but it will make me look better if I tell them myself. You know, noble.

JESSE: Oh . . . so, what is it?

SAMMY: I'm going to be suspended.

JESSE: From school?

SAMMY: No, from dinner. Of course school, you moron.

JESSE: Oh wow. Suspended. When?

SAMMY: As of 11:30 this morning.

JESSE: This morning? You were suspended this morning?

SAMMY: Uh huh.

JESSE: It's 4:00 now. Where have you been all day?

SAMMY: At the show.

JESSE: Oh, fine. First you get suspended, then you spend all day at the show without permission. What did you see?

SAMMY: I really don't think that is the issue at this point.

JESSE: You saw something "R" rated, didn't you? First suspended, now "R" rated movies. What next?

SAMMY: You are out of your mind. You are an idiot. Why did I even think that I could confide in you? You are so stupid. What movie I saw today has no bearing on the fact that I was suspended from school. God!!!

JESSE: I'm sorry. I guess I just got carried away. OK, I'm fine now. What were you suspended for, anyway?

SAMMY: I cut Biology.

JESSE: You cut Biology, and they suspended you? For that? I think they over-reacted a little, don't you?

SAMMY: It was the thirteenth cut.

JESSE: *(Loudly)* **You cut a class thirteen times?**

SAMMY: I hate science.

JESSE: But you cut . . . thirteen times. Why? How?

SAMMY: I told you, I hate science.

JESSE: No, I mean how did you get away with it twelve times?

SAMMY: Apparently, I didn't.

JESSE: I don't understand.

SAMMY: Well, at first I would leave for just a few minutes during the middle of the period, you know, with a pass to go to the bathroom.

JESSE: Yeah, I know.

SAMMY: Then I started to stay longer than just a few minutes . . . and then I started to leave at the beginning of the period . . but I had the pass.

JESSE: So what went wrong?

SAMMY: The jerk started to pay attention to how long I was gone and then, behind my back, without even telling me, he counted my going to the bathroom as cutting his class.

JESSE: *(Sarcastically)* **The nerve.**

SAMMY: Don't be an idiot, whose side are you on here, anyway?

JESSE: There is no side. You cut his class.

SAMMY: I was there for roll.

JESSE: Yeah, but you left right after and missed the whole class.

SAMMY: I came back.

JESSE: Forty-five minutes after the class started.

SAMMY: I don't even know why we have to take science. I'm never going to use it. You don't need science to work in the film industry.

JESSE: I hate when you talk like that.

SAMMY: Like what?

JESSE: "The film industry." You sound like a jerk.

SAMMY: You're the jerk.

JESSE: Yeah? Well, I'm not the one who just got suspended from school for cutting *(Loudly)* **THIRTEEN TIMES, now am I?**

SAMMY: Shut up before mom comes in here. I knew I shouldn't tell you. I hate you sometimes.

MOM: *(Off-stage)* **Is there a problem in there, kids?**

TOGETHER: No, Mom.

MOM: *(Off-stage)* **Then quit yelling. I'm trying to work.**

TOGETHER: OK, Mom. *(There is a brief pause while SAMMY and JESSE look at each other.)*

JESSE: What are you going to do?

SAMMY: Heck, I don't know.

JESSE: You want me to go in with you?

SAMMY: No. I don't want to tell her.

JESSE: Good luck.

SAMMY: *(On way out)* **Thanks.**

JESSE: If she kills you, can I have your room?

SAMMY: *(Half-hearted smile before exit.)* **Sure.**

JESSE: See ya.

SAMMY: See ya. *(Exits.)*

TAKING A JOKE

MATT: 17, in love and miserable.

EMILY: Also 17, is Matt's best friend, but would like to be more.

SETTING: Setting up stage for a rehearsal of Odd Couple, taking chairs, tables, etc. and placing them in the position the actors will use.

MATT: *(Arranging two chairs)* **Emily, will you hurry up?**

EMILY: *(Entering, carrying a box loaded with hand props)* **I'm moving as fast as I can. And by the way, I'd like to thank you for all of your help.**

MATT: Just set it down and stop complaining. I swear, all I ever get from anybody these days is complaints.

EMILY: Matt, I was just kidding.

MATT: Well, to be completely honest . . . I'm not in a kidding mood, OK?

EMILY: OK. *(She begins to place props in position while MATT arranges chairs and table. This business will go on for the entire scene.)* **So. How are you?**

MATT: Fine.

EMILY: *(A beat)* **I'm fine, too.**

MATT: Good.

EMILY: *(A beat)* **You going out tonight?**

MATT: No.

EMILY: *(A beat)* **I'm not going out, either.**

MATT: Oh.

EMILY: *(After a pause)* **So, how about those Knicks?**

MATT: *(Displaying some irritation)* **What?**

EMILY: Nothing. *(They continue to set up the scene, EMILY glancing now and then at MATT for some clue as to his emotional state.)* **Is Rachel coming to pick you up after rehearsal?**

MATT: No.

EMILY: *(With understanding)* **Oh.**

MATT: And what does that mean? What does "Oh" mean?

EMILY: Oh means Oh. That's all, just Oh. A generic Oh.

MATT: Emily, I know that we are friends, but I just don't need this right now.

EMILY: Need what? I just said "Oh."

MATT: I talk to you too much. I need to keep some things to myself.

EMILY: I said "Oh". I never asked you anything. Keep what you want to yourself.

MATT: Emily, you don't have to get mad. It's just that I'm going through some things that I need to think through.

EMILY: What, for instance?

MATT: I don't know if I can tell you. I don't know how to tell you.

EMILY: Just say it.

MATT: It's something that I've never said to anyone before.

EMILY: Matt, we've known each other since first grade. We have experienced everything from jungle gyms to puberty together. Nothing you can tell me can surprise me. I know about every girl you've ever gone out with and you know about every guy I've ever gone out with . . . all two of them.

MATT: But this is different. I've never felt this before for anyone.

EMILY: Matt, don't be shy, just say what is in your heart.

MATT: I think I'm in love with Rachel.

EMILY: So I was wrong . . . I'm surprised. Why Rachel? I mean, she is not the nicest person in the world.

MATT: Emily, don't start. I know she's not your favorite person, but she happens to be very special to me.

EMILY: Why should I say anything bad about her? I mean it's not like she has ever stood you up on a date. It's been at least a week since she told you you were stupid. I know it's been at least that long since she let Richie Hall drive her home from school and then let him come in the house while her parents were out. He seemed to have quite the conversation going with her the next day.

MATT: Stop it, Emily.

EMILY: I thought they looked rather cute together. Heads bowed close, secret shared smiles.

MATT: I told you Monday that she explained that. They were just working on a scene together for class. That was all it was.

EMILY: Ah.

MATT: Don't give me "Ah," Emily.

EMILY: Then let me give you some advice. Lose this chick.

MATT: I told you, I'm in love with her.

EMILY: No you're not. You're in love with the idea of being in love with a dream.

MATT: OK, Sigmund Freud, what does that mean?

EMILY: It means that you always want what you can't have. Always. You're just like Scarlett O'Hara.

MATT: What?

EMILY: Remember that part when Melanie is dying and Scarlett realizes she could now have Ashley?

MATT: I never read the book.

EMILY: The movie is the same way in that part.

MATT: I never saw it.

EMILY: YOU'VE NEVER SEEN GONE WITH THE WIND? We've been friends since birth and you've kept this secret from me?

MATT: What's your point, Emily?

EMILY: My point, Matthew, is that you, not unlike

Scarlett O'Hara, only want what you can't have.

MATT: I don't understand.

EMILY: Read the book.

MATT: I don't have time. Explain yourself.

EMILY: You, my ignorant friend, have the unfortunate habit of going for girls that will crap all over you, make you look like a fool, and laugh with their friends when you come crawling back for more.

MATT: Thank you so much.

EMILY: I'm serious, they do.

MATT: But Rachel is different when we're alone. She told me she loves me.

EMILY: God, you're stupid.

MATT: Thank you so much.

EMILY: Didn't you wonder what people were smirking about last week when you would walk by?

MATT: No, I didn't notice.

EMILY: Right. I was with you and I saw you notice, you just ignored. But it's eating you up.

MATT: What is eating me up?

EMILY: The fact that this girl treats you like the lowest life form and everyone knows it and you just take it.

MATT: I love her. I know that she treats me like crap as you so elegantly put it, but I love her.

EMILY: And, also like Scarlett, you ignore what is right in front of you.

MATT: What do you mean?

EMILY: Did it ever occur to you that I might care about you?

MATT: Emily, please don't say that.

EMILY: Why?

MATT: Don't tell me that. Don't do this.

EMILY: Do what?

MATT: Turn our friendship inside out.

EMILY: What do you mean?

MATT: I don't need another girlfriend. I need a friend, and you are the best one I have.

EMILY: Isn't that what I am?

MATT: No, you are not my girlfriend. You are my best friend who happens to be a girl.

EMILY: You are a walking ego, you know that?

MATT: I don't understand.

EMILY: You think every girl, except of course for Miss Barracuda USA, is in love with you.

MATT: What are you saying?

EMILY: I was joking, for heaven's sake. God, you are really wrapped up in yourself, aren't you?

MATT: Are you serious? You were joking?

EMILY: I figured you needed something to laugh about, and I decided on the most ludicrous subject . . . you and me together as a couple. It was a joke, jerk.

MATT: Well, I am embarrassed.

EMILY: You should be. Give me some credit, please.

MATT: That is funny, though. You and me as a couple. I mean, picture it, we took baths together when we were kids.

EMILY: I know. Funny, huh?

MATT: Remember all the times we spent the night at each other's house?

EMILY: Remember how we cried when our moms said we couldn't do that anymore?

MATT: And then the next day we compared notes on the birds and bees talk they gave us?

EMILY: God, we were young.

MATT: I'm glad you're my friend.

EMILY: Me, too.

MATT: Don't ever change, OK?

EMILY: I never will. *(Hugs him.)*

MATT: I think we're all set up here. I'll tell everyone we're ready.

EMILY: Do you feel any better?

MATT: Honestly, no. But I laughed, at least for a second or two.

EMILY: Call me tonight, after rehearsal, we can talk. Maybe I can talk some sense into you about this . . .

MATT: Don't say anything bad about her. I'm in love.

EMILY: You're a fool.

MATT: I'll call you tonight.

EMILY: You do that. We can discuss your ego. *(He leaves.)* **I am a fool. I am a fool. I am a fool.**

BLIND DATE

SUSI: Attractive teen, sure of herself, confident, thoughtful of other's feelings.

SUSAN: Susi's alter ego. Says what Susi wishes she could say, is apparent only to audience.

HANK: Arrogant, sure of himself, but for no apparent reason. He is every girl's nightmare of a blind date.

HENRY: Hank's alter ego. Even worse than Hank.

SETTING: The script has several minor scene changes which will involve the use of a table and two chairs. The Alter Egos make the scene changes while Susi and Hank move into them.

SCENE 1
AT THE MIRROR

(SUSI and HANK are off Center-stage a little bit facing to the wings. SUSAN and HENRY face them, mirroring their movements.)

HANK: *(Putting on garish shirt, tucking it into too short slacks.)* **Perfect. Yes indeed. That Susi girl is going to love this Ensemble.** *(Pronounce On Sowm)*

SUSI: *(Putting on finishing touches of make-up)* **Oh Lordy, Oh Lordy, please don't make this guy a geek.**

HANK: *(Slicking back hair)* **Hair looks good. Can almost see yourself in the reflection. Too cool.**

SUSI: It's going to be a disaster. All blind dates are a disaster. Why did I agree to this?

HANK: Oh, you lucky girl. I hope you appreciate the prize that is about to arrive at your front door.

SUSI: *(One last look in the mirror)* **I guess I look OK. This dress isn't as dressy as I'd like.**

HANK: Hold on, baby, because here comes Hanky. OOOWWW!!!

SCENE 2
AT THE DOOR

(Heads are down to indicate new scene. Actors turn, HANK and HENRY cross to SUSI and SUSAN's playing area. HANK pantomimes knocking at door. When the alter egos talk, the characters of SUSI and HANK should not look at them. They should only register a small facial reaction, as when you normally do when thinking of things. This should NOT be overdone!)

HENRY: OK, baby, just be cool. You are the best. Hair looks good, clothes are stylin'. Personality to spare.

SUSAN: Take a deep breath. Just go out there. Answer the door and make yourself have a good time. How bad can it be? Sheila is a good friend and she wouldn't fix you up with a complete geek. *(SUSI goes to door, answers it. HENRY and SUSAN crane around to get a look at SUSI and HANK.)*

SUSAN: *(In horror)* **Omigod!**

HENRY: *(Said at the same time and in admiration.)* **Omigod!**

SUSI: *(Covering shock nicely)* **Well, I assume you are Hank?**

SUSAN: Please say no. *(Quietly)* **pleasepleasepleaseplease.**

HANK: You got it baby.

HENRY: The big score, Hanky baby.

SUSAN: Oh God, no. I can't believe it. Sheila is a dead woman.

HENRY: Mental note to send cousin Sheila bon bons tomorrow.

SUSI: It's so nice to meet you. You know, Sheila didn't really tell me that much about you.

HANK: Savin' it for a surprise, I guess. My cousin loves to give people a shock.

HENRY: And I'm having cardiac arrest. What a babe.

SUSAN: Shock, heck, I'm having a heart attack. Before I die, she goes. Torture, maiming, fixing her up with

my geek cousin. The works.

SUSI: Shall we go?

HENRY: She's hot for you Hanky. She can't wait to get you alone.

SUSAN: Let's get this evening over with as quickly as possible. One quick meal, preferably someplace dark, and then home.

HANK: I know a great little club. Do you have a fake ID?

SUSAN: Not to waste on you. Besides, my friends might see me with this jerk.

SUSI: Oh, no, I don't.

HENRY: Just as well. That club costs bucks. One quick meal, and then, zip, backseat time.

HANK: Hey, baby, no problem. We'll go someplace fine, to suit your fine looks.

SUSI: *(Smiles uneasily)*

SUSAN: I'm going to be sick.

HENRY: I am just too cool tonight.

HANK: Let me walk behind you for a minute, so I can see a dream walking.

HENRY: Oh, too cool.

SUSAN: Definitely going to be sick.

SCENE 3
THE PUB

(SUSAN and HENRY have set up a small table and two chairs. They can also sit in chairs or stand, depending on director's blocking.)

HANK: Nice place, huh? Cozy. *(Scoots chair closer to her)*

SUSI: *(Moving away slightly, but not so much as to offend)* **A little dark.** *(She squints, looking around.)*

SUSAN: *(Also squinting and looking around)* **Dark enough to not be seen with you, but still light enough to see you.**

HENRY: Put your arm around her. Do the old yawn and stretch.

HANK: Whew, long day, huh?

SUSI: Yes, it was.

SUSAN: Why does each minute seem to drag?

HANK: *(Signaling to a waiter)* **Some potato chips and two beers over here.**

SUSAN: Last of the Big Time Spenders.

SUSI: *(Whispering)* **I told you I didn't have an I.D.**

HANK: No problem, they know me here. *(Looking off)* **What? Oh, that's OK. Make it two cokes.**

HENRY: *(Indicating waiter)* **What a jerk.**

SUSAN: *(Indicating HANK)* **What a jerk.**

HENRY: So, let's make with some sweet talk.

HANK: So, babe, after we're finished here, let's do some backseat talkin'.

HENRY: Yes, yes, yes.

SUSI and SUSAN: Omigod!

HANK: Sounds good to you, too, huh?

SUSI: Could you please move over?

SUSAN: Preferably into the next county.

HENRY: Closer and closer.

HANK: Anything you say.

SUSI: I meant the other way.

HANK: Is there a problem?

SUSI: I think we should go.

HENRY: I told you, she can't wait.

HANK: Great idea.

SCENE 4
IN THE CAR ON THE WAY HOME

(The two dining chairs now serve as the front seat of a car. SUSAN and HENRY sit above or stand above SUSI and HANK.)

HENRY: Make your move, boy. Pull the car over. Park!

SUSAN: Just let me get home. Just let me get home. Just let me get home.

HANK: Oh. Hey. What's the matter with this car? I just better pull on over.

SUSAN: Oh no. Please, not this. Sheila, I swear, you are a dead woman.

HENRY: Ooohh. Back seat lovin', here I come.

HANK: I think it's just overheating. We'll just sit here for a while and let it cool off.

SUSI: Are you sure?

HENRY: Listen to how eager she is.

HANK: No choice, babe.

SUSAN: That's it, brother. We're walking home. I've had about all I can take for one evening.

SUSI: You know what, Hank, it's been a long day, and I think that I'll just walk home from here. It's not that far and I'll be fine.

SUSAN: Even a mugger would be a step up from this guy.

HENRY: Oh, she wants to walk in the moonlight.

HANK: Why don't we just wait here for the car to cool off?

HENRY: Quick thinking!

HANK: It's nice and cozy and we can get to know each other real good.

SUSAN: I'm going to gag. That's it. I've reached my gag level.

SUSI: No, really, it's OK.

HANK: *(Trying to make his move)* **Now, babe, I know you want me real bad.**

SUSAN and SUSI: What did you say?

HENRY and HANK: No use fighting it.

HANK: Give in to the feeling.

SUSAN: You sickening turd.

SUSI: Listen, Hank, for the sake of Sheila's friendship,

let's not go too far. We both might regret what will happen.

HENRY: She wants you. She wants you bad.

HANK: Go with it babe, just go with it.

SUSAN: OMIGOD! Sheila is history. Call Rose Hills, 'cause a body is on its way. This guy is the biggest jerk on earth.

SUSI: Listen, Hank. I've tried to be as nice as I could be. I'm really a very nice person . .

SUSAN: Which is why these things happen to me . . .

SUSI: But I can't take this anymore, so I'm going to leave you now. Do you understand?

HENRY: She can hardly control herself.

HANK: *(Totally cool)* **I can dig it, babe. Hey . . . I'll call you.**

SUSAN and SUSI: What?

HANK: I'll give you a call . . . maybe tomorrow . . . maybe the next day.

HENRY: Yeah, keep her hanging.

SUSI: No, wait. I'll call you.

SUSAN: That number gets burned the second I get home. Along with Sheila's.

HENRY: She can't stand the thought of waiting. She wants to be the one to call. This is great.

HANK: Sure. Whatever, babe.

SUSAN: The name is NOT babe, you creep.

SUSI: Fine. Well, good luck with the car, and you'll hear from me . . .

SUSAN: As soon as hell freezes over.

HANK: Great, babe. Talk to ya. *(As SUSAN and SUSI walk away, all four say:)*

SUSAN and SUSI: *(In complete disgust)* **What a night!**

HENRY and HANK: *(In absolute heaven)* **What a night!**

ABOUT THE AUTHOR

Mary Krell-Oishi has been teaching since 1976 and began her high school theatre teaching at Sunny Hills High School in Fullerton, California, in 1984. She recently completed her Masters in Theatre Education at California State University, Fullerton and has absolutely no plans whatsoever to pursue a higher degree. One is enough, thank you very much.

Her primary career joy has been and remains teaching high school theatre and interacting with young, fresh talent. Mrs. Krell-Oishi takes great pride in the fact she was named as Playwright of the Year by the California State Thespians at their conference in 1995. Her plans are to continue working with high school drama student and to focus her writing for them.

Mary lives with her husband Harris, son Richard and cat D.C. in Yorba Linda, California.

Order Form

Meriwether Publishing Ltd.
PO Box 7710
Colorado Springs CO 80933-7710
Phone: 800-937-5297 Fax: 719-594-9916
Website: www.meriwether.com

Please send me the following books:

________ **Scenes That Happen #BK-B156** **$15.95**
by Mary Krell-Oishi
Dramatized snapshots of high school life

________ **Scenes Keep Happening #BK-B280** **$15.95**
by Mary Krell-Oishi
More real-life snapshots of teen lives

________ **More Scenes That Happen #BK-B112** **$14.95**
by Mary Krell-Oishi
More real-life snapshots of teenage lives

________ **Perspectives #BK-B206** **$14.95**
by Mary Krell-Oishi
Relevant scenes for teens

________ **Winning Monologs for Young Actors #BK-B127** **$15.95**
by Peg Kehret
Honest-to-life monologs for young actors

________ **Encore! More Winning Monologs for Young Actors #BK-B144** **$15.95**
by Peg Kehret
More honest-to-life monologs for young actors

________ **The Flip Side #BK-B221** **$15.95**
by Heather H. Henderson
64 point-of-view monologs for teens

These and other fine Meriwether Publishing books are available at your local bookstore or direct from the publisher. Prices subject to change without notice. Check our website or call for current prices.

Name: ____________________ e-mail: ________________

Organization name: ____________________________

Address: __________________________________

City: _________________________ State: ____________

Zip: ____________________ Phone: ________________

❑ **Check enclosed**

❑ **Visa / MasterCard / Discover #** ________________________

Signature: ________________________ *Expiration date:* ____________
(required for credit card orders)

Colorado residents: Please add 3% sales tax.
Shipping: Include $3.95 for the first book and 75¢ for each additional book ordered.

❑ *Please send me a copy of your complete catalog of books and plays.*